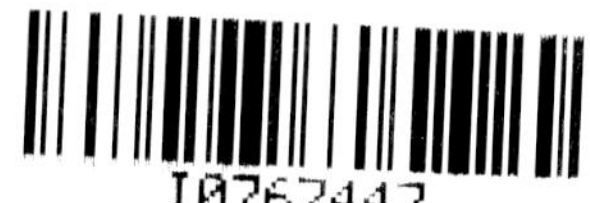
I0767447

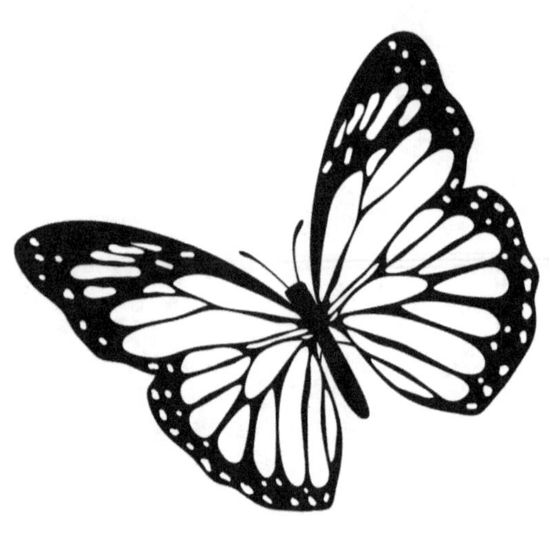

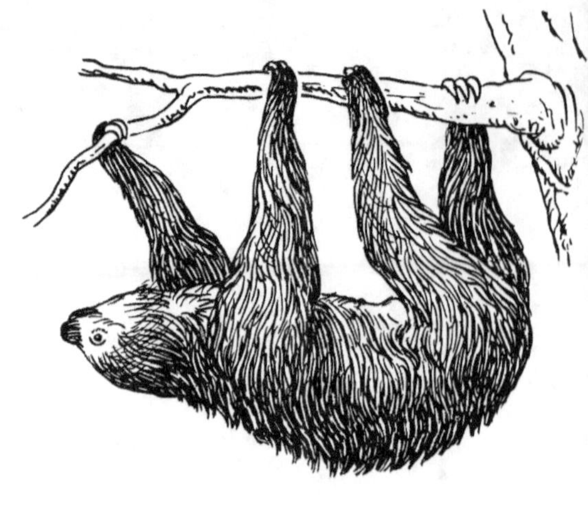

This Book Belongs to:

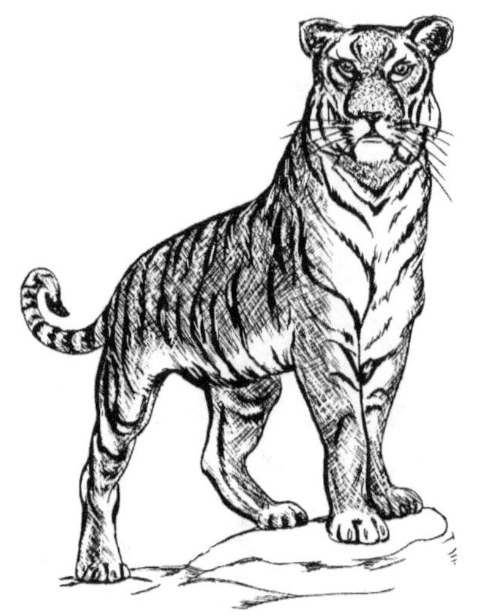

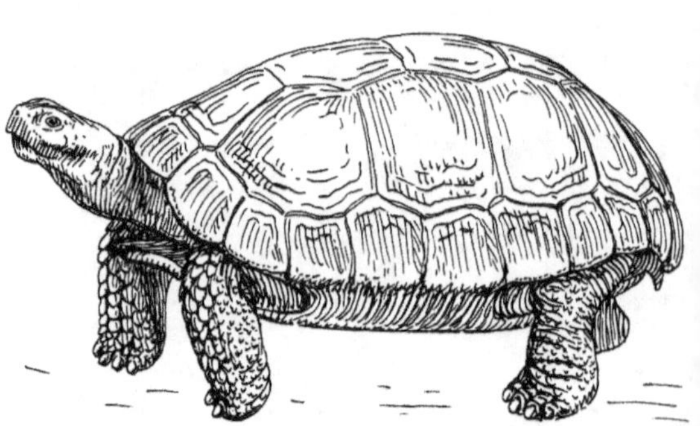

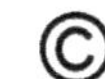

Test Color Page

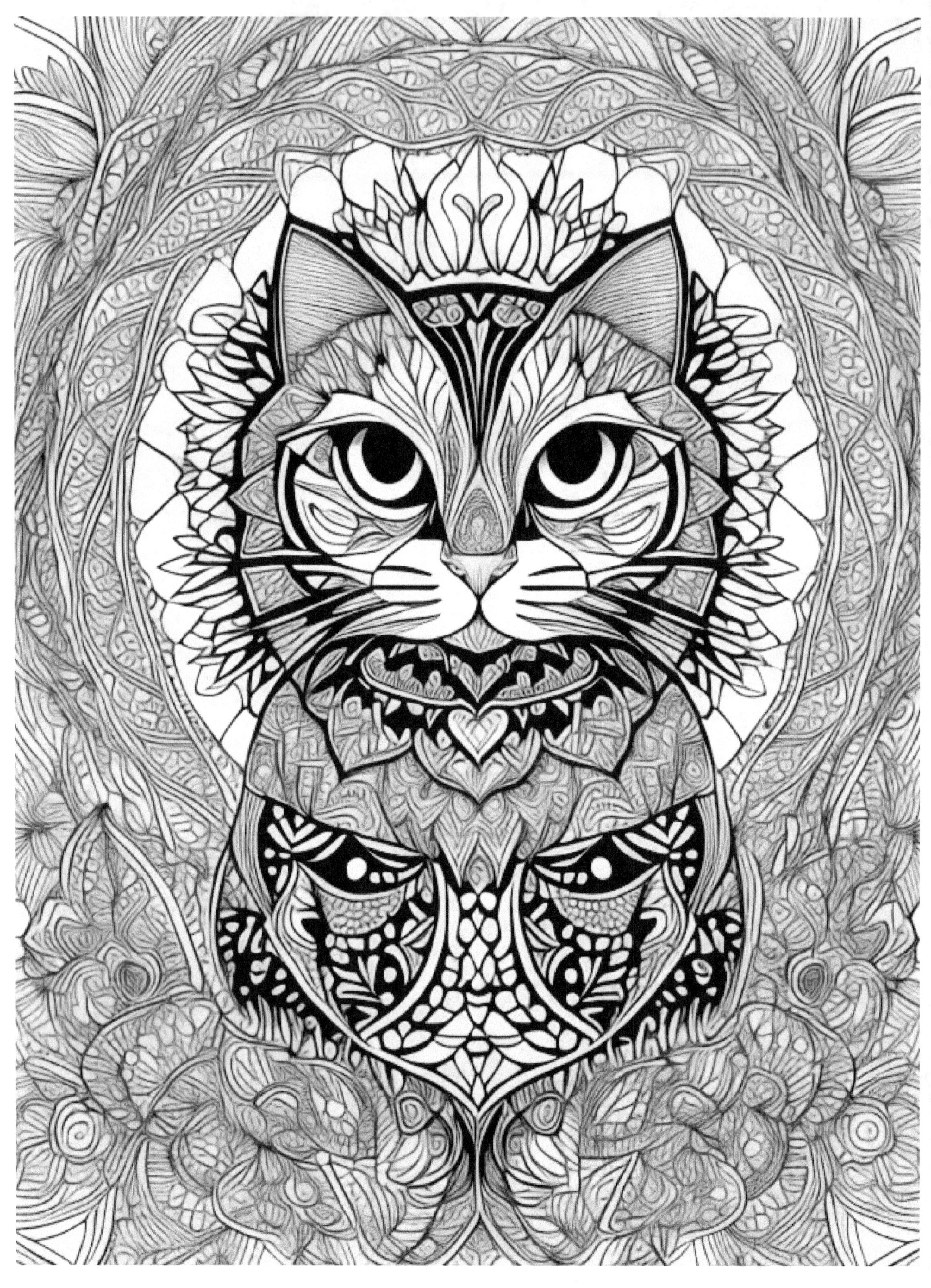

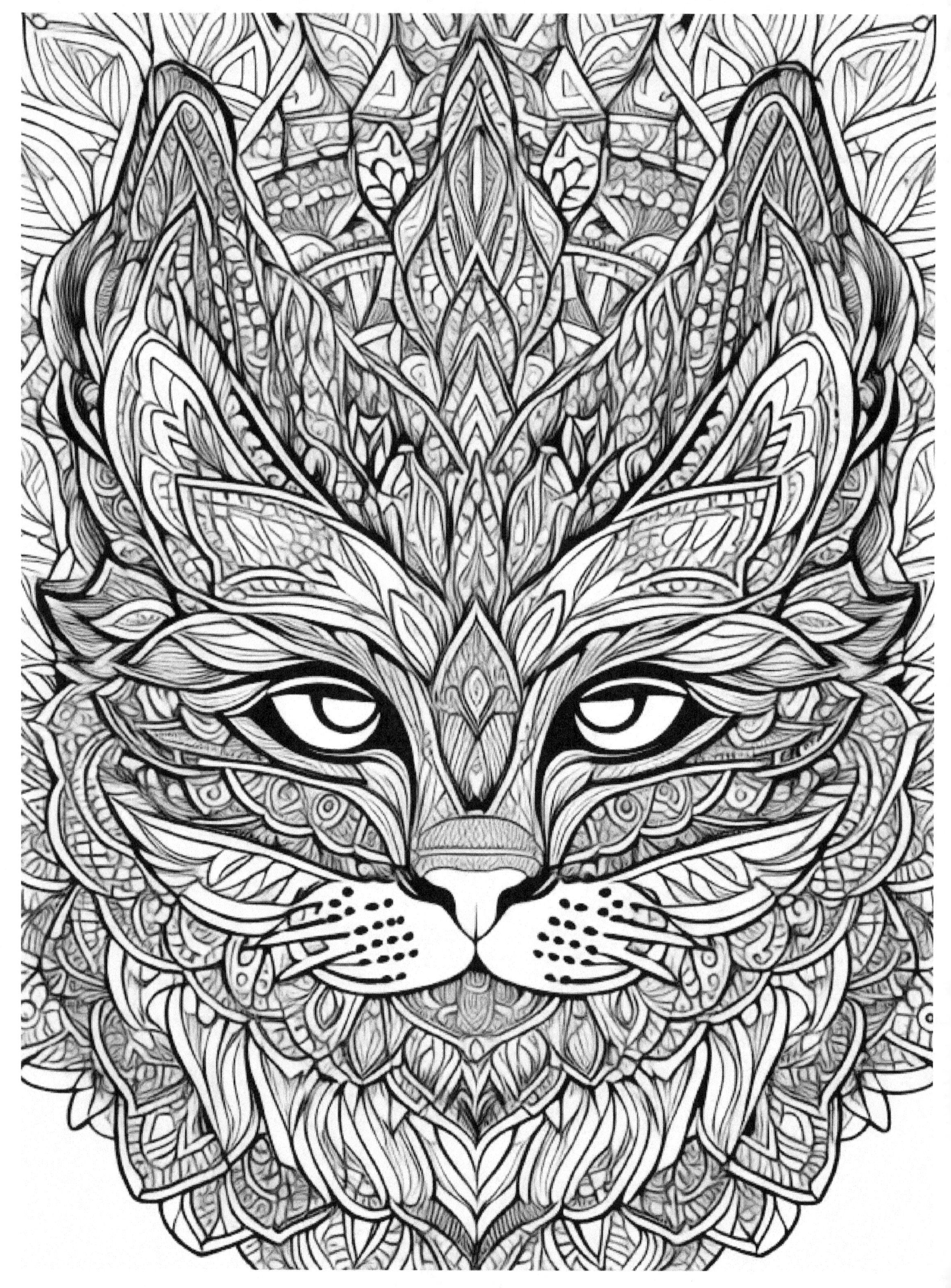

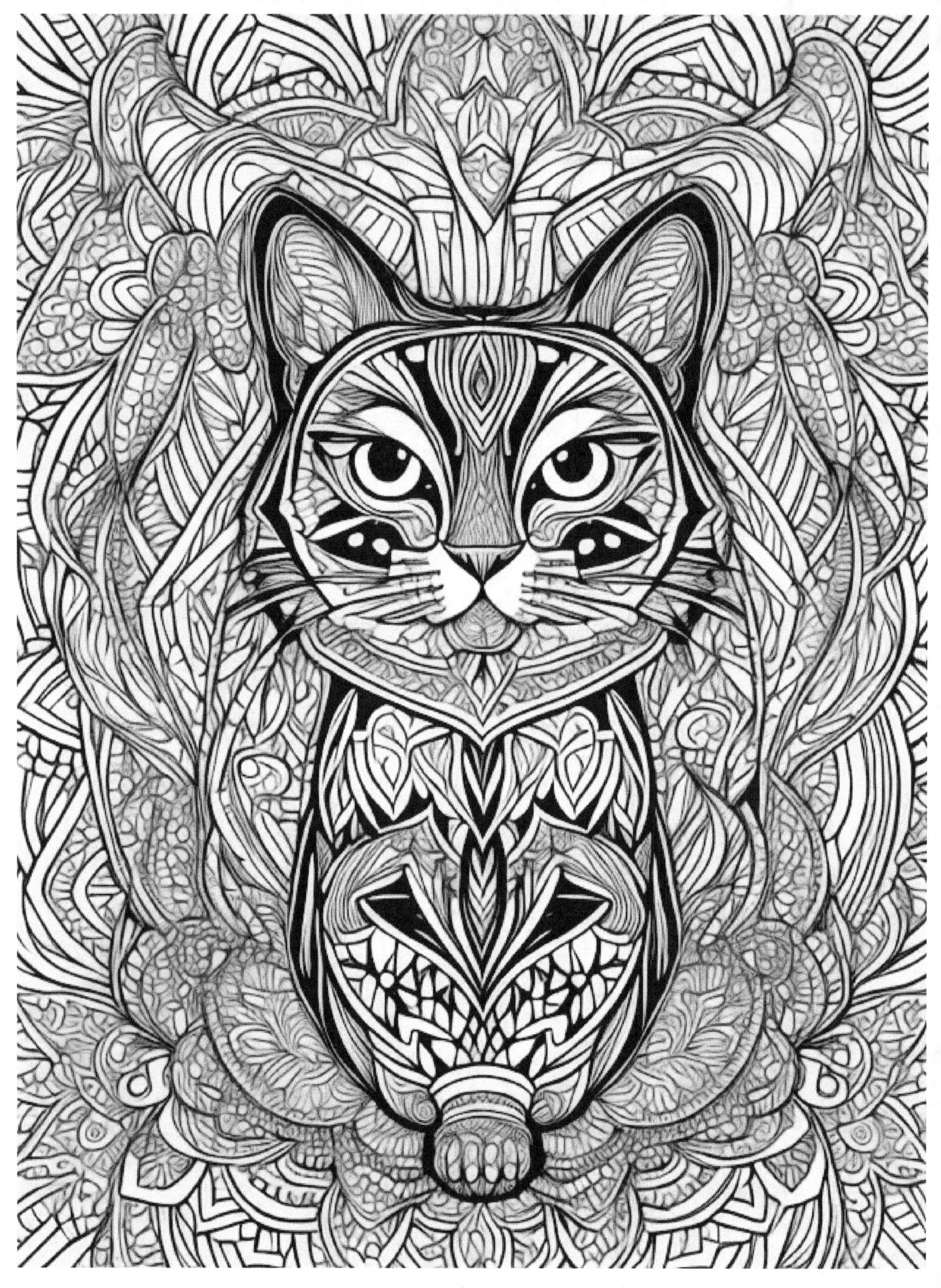

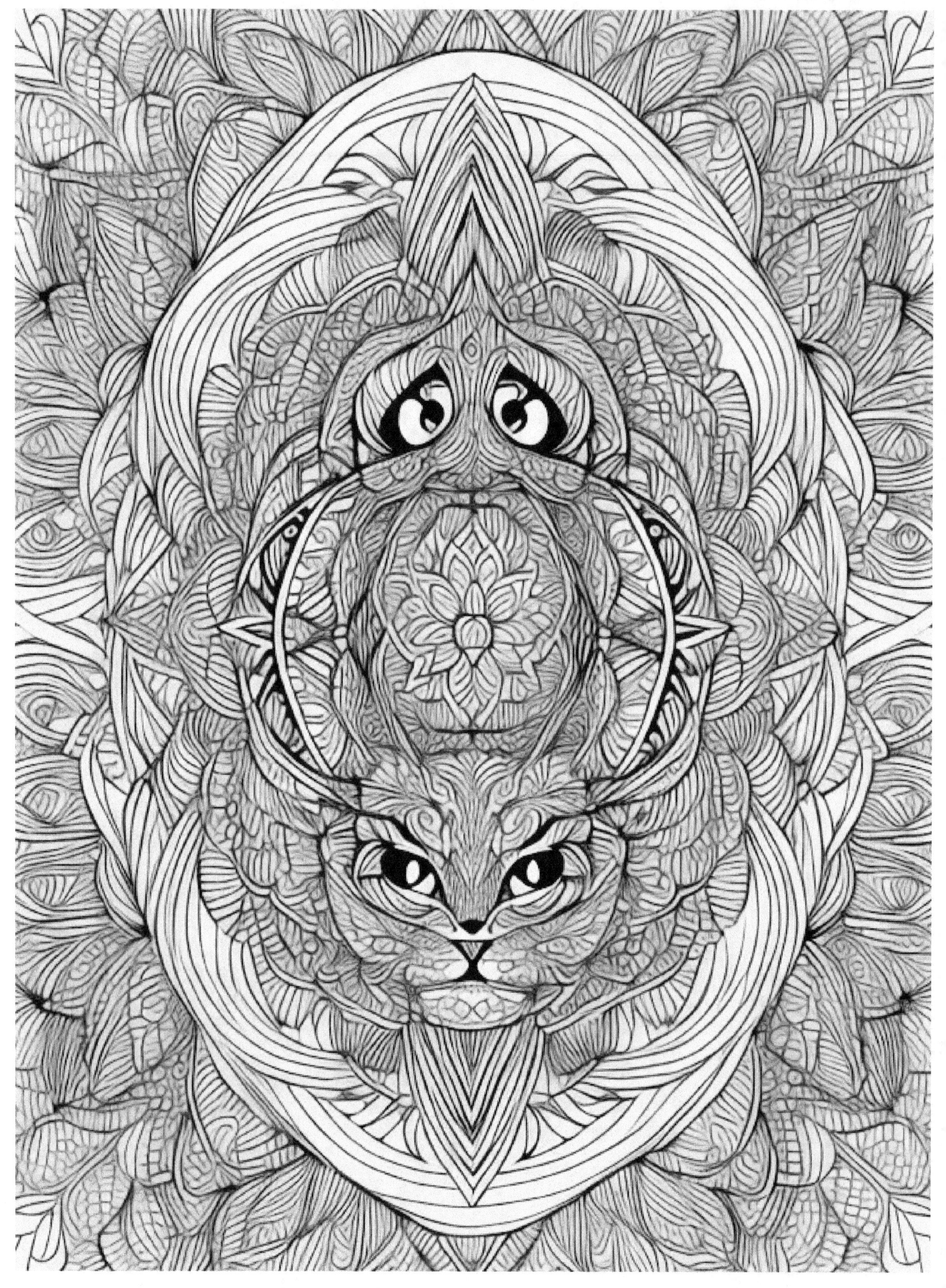

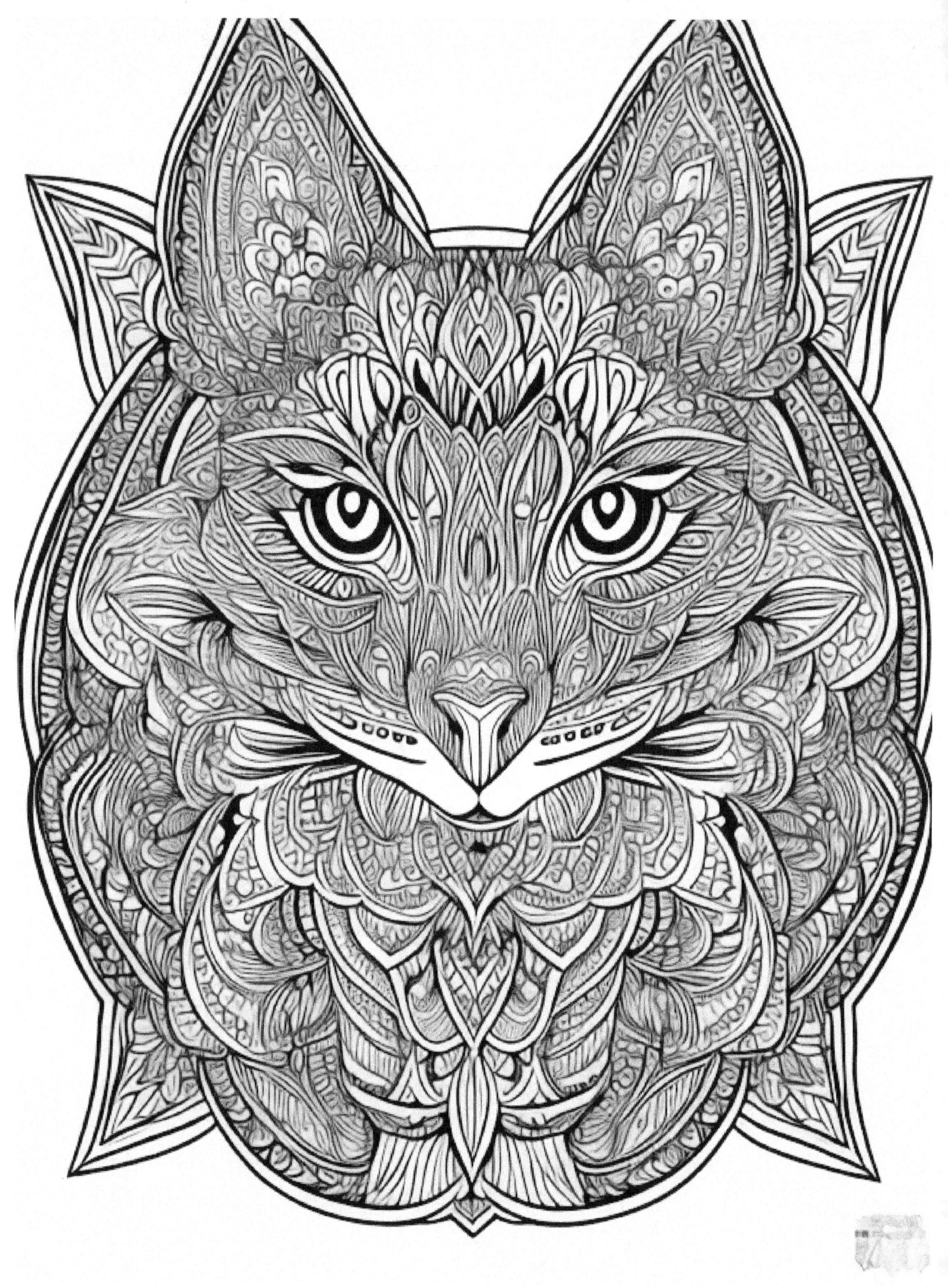

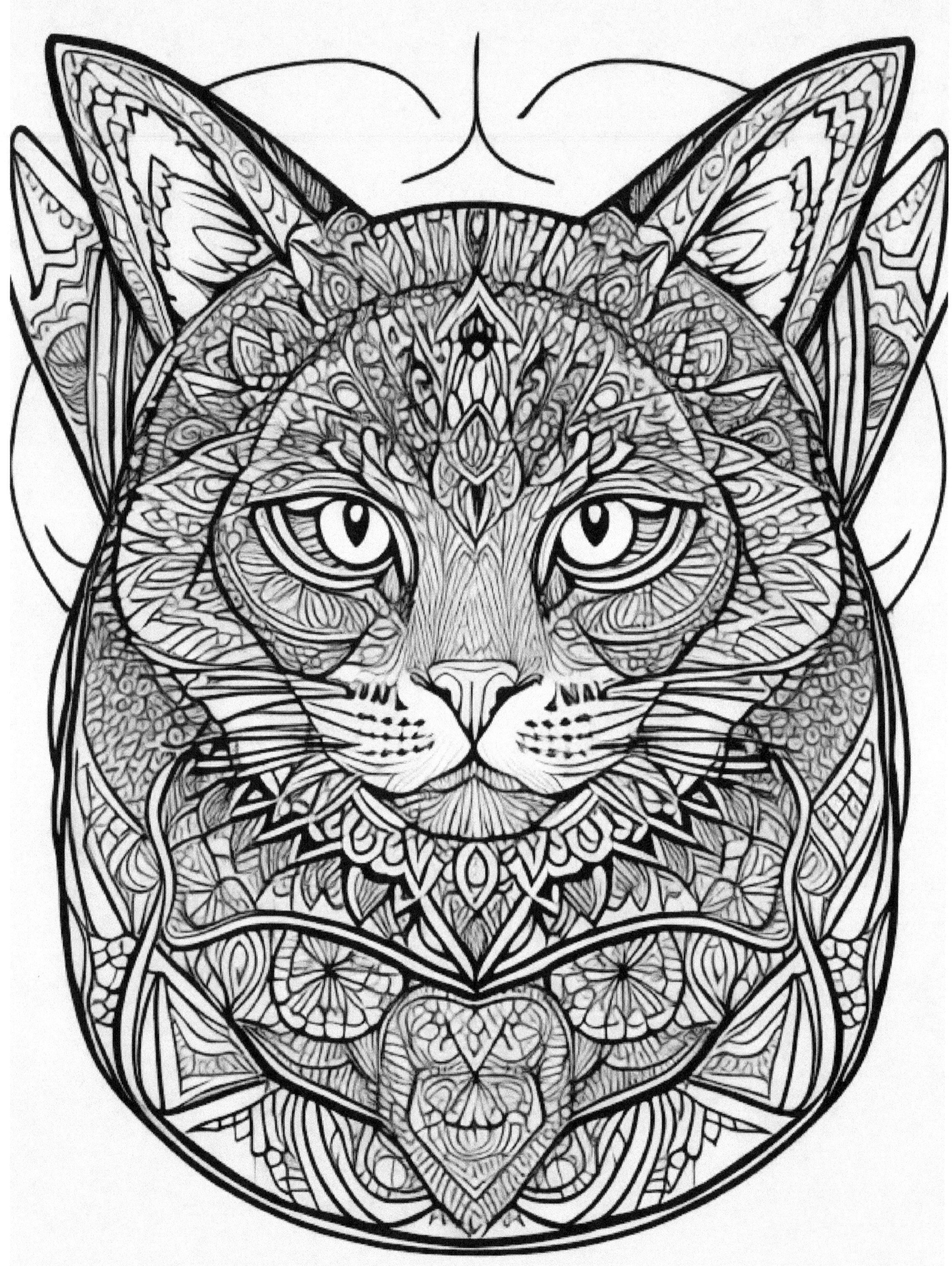

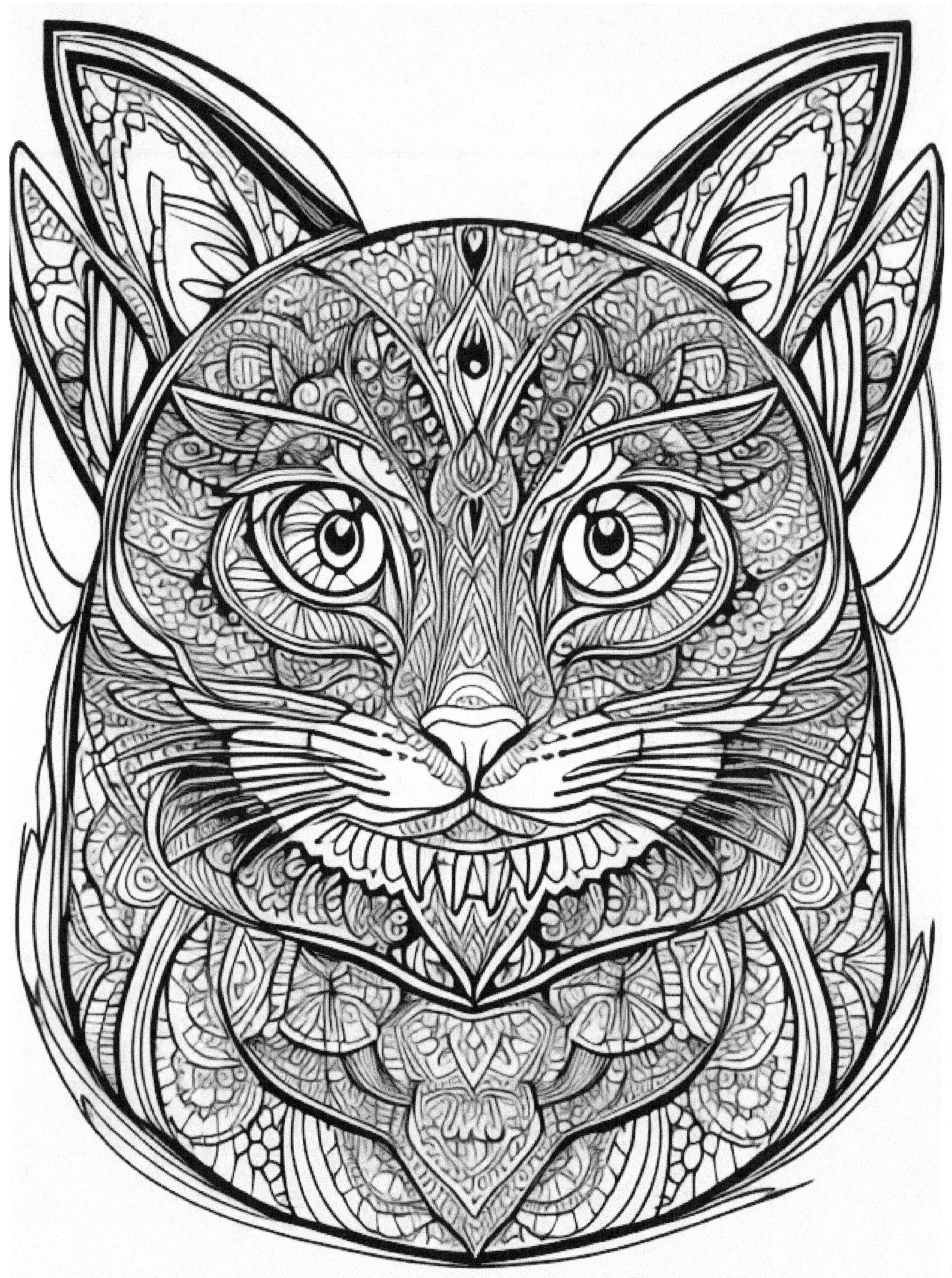

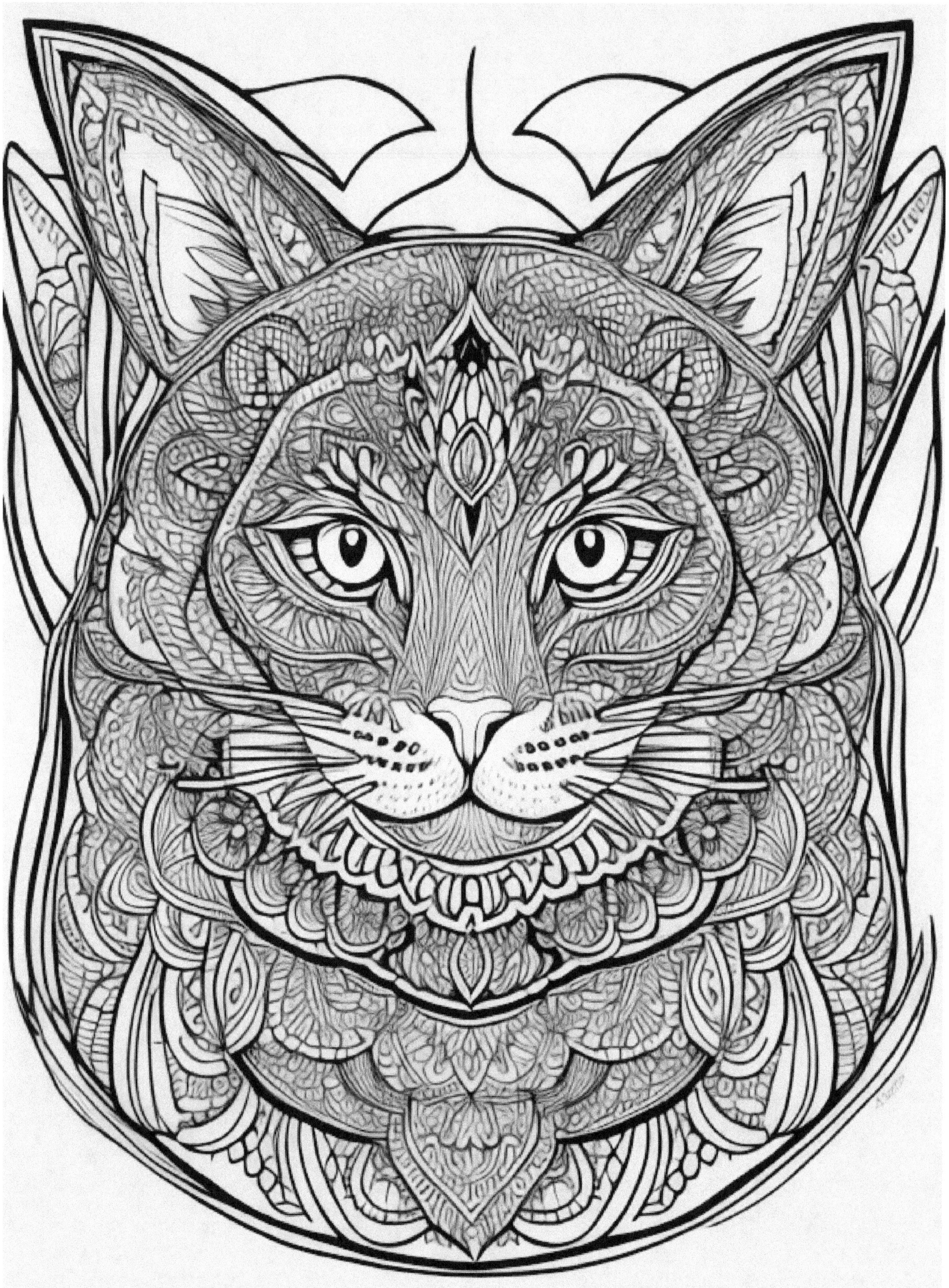

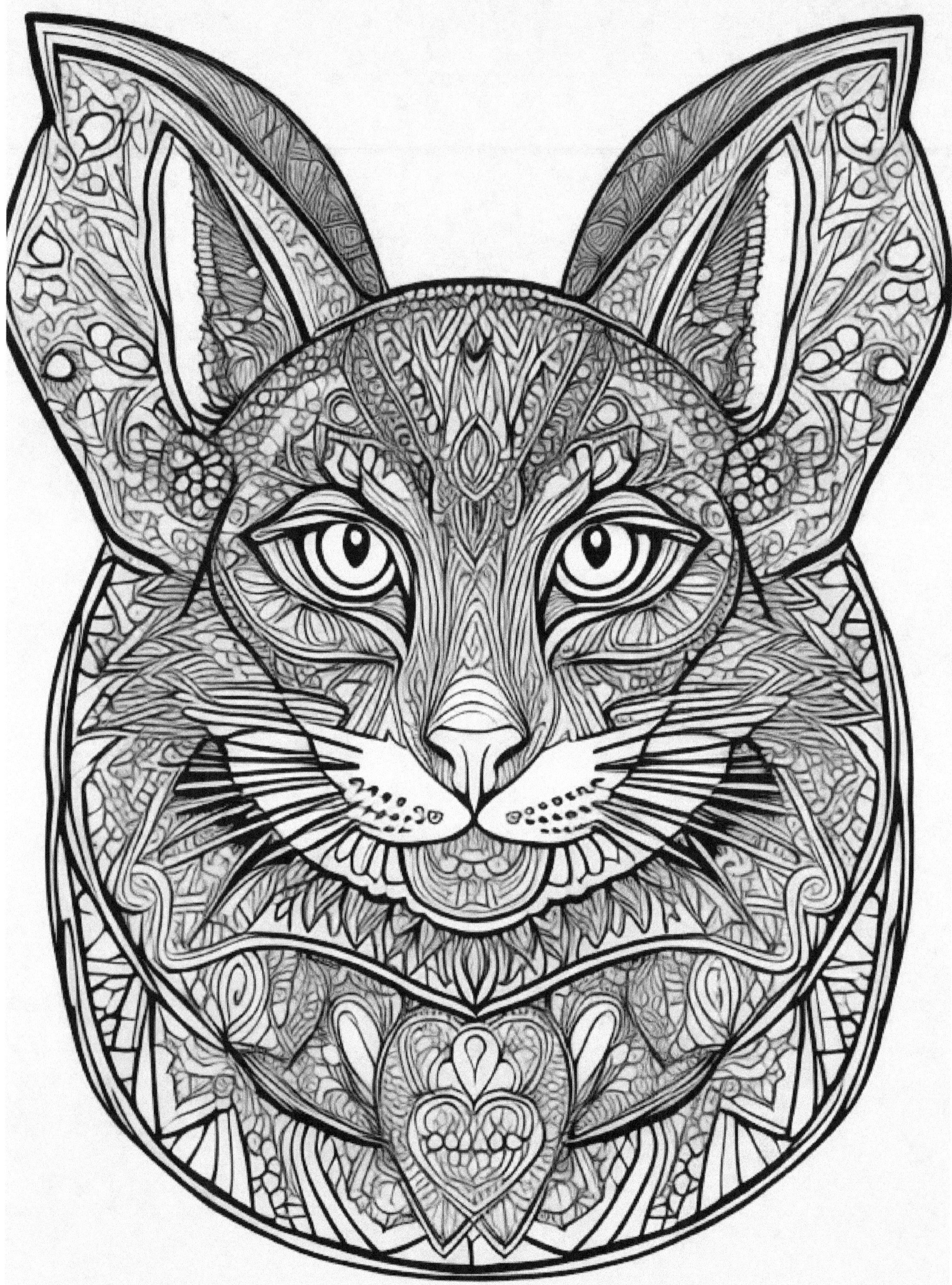

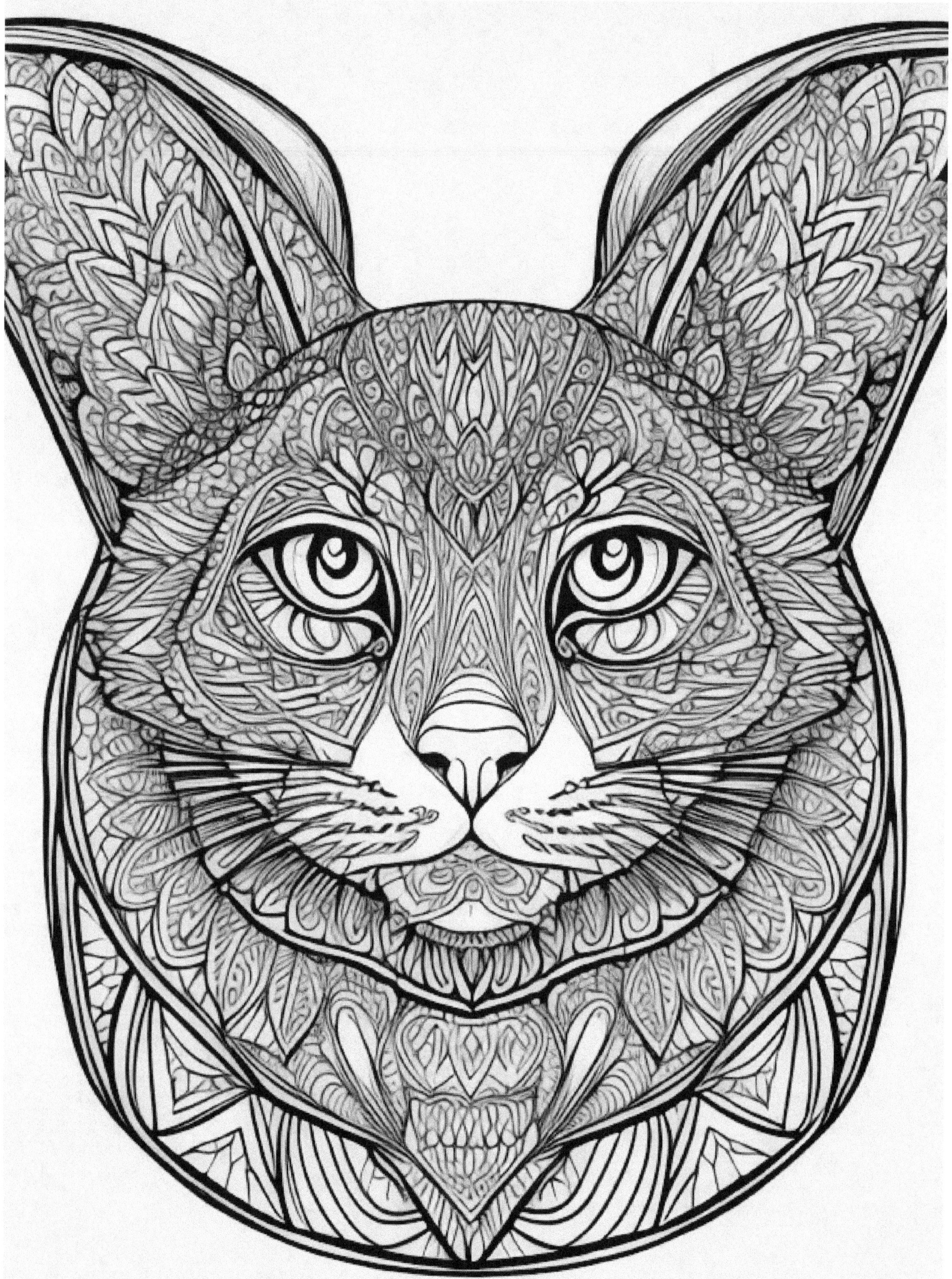

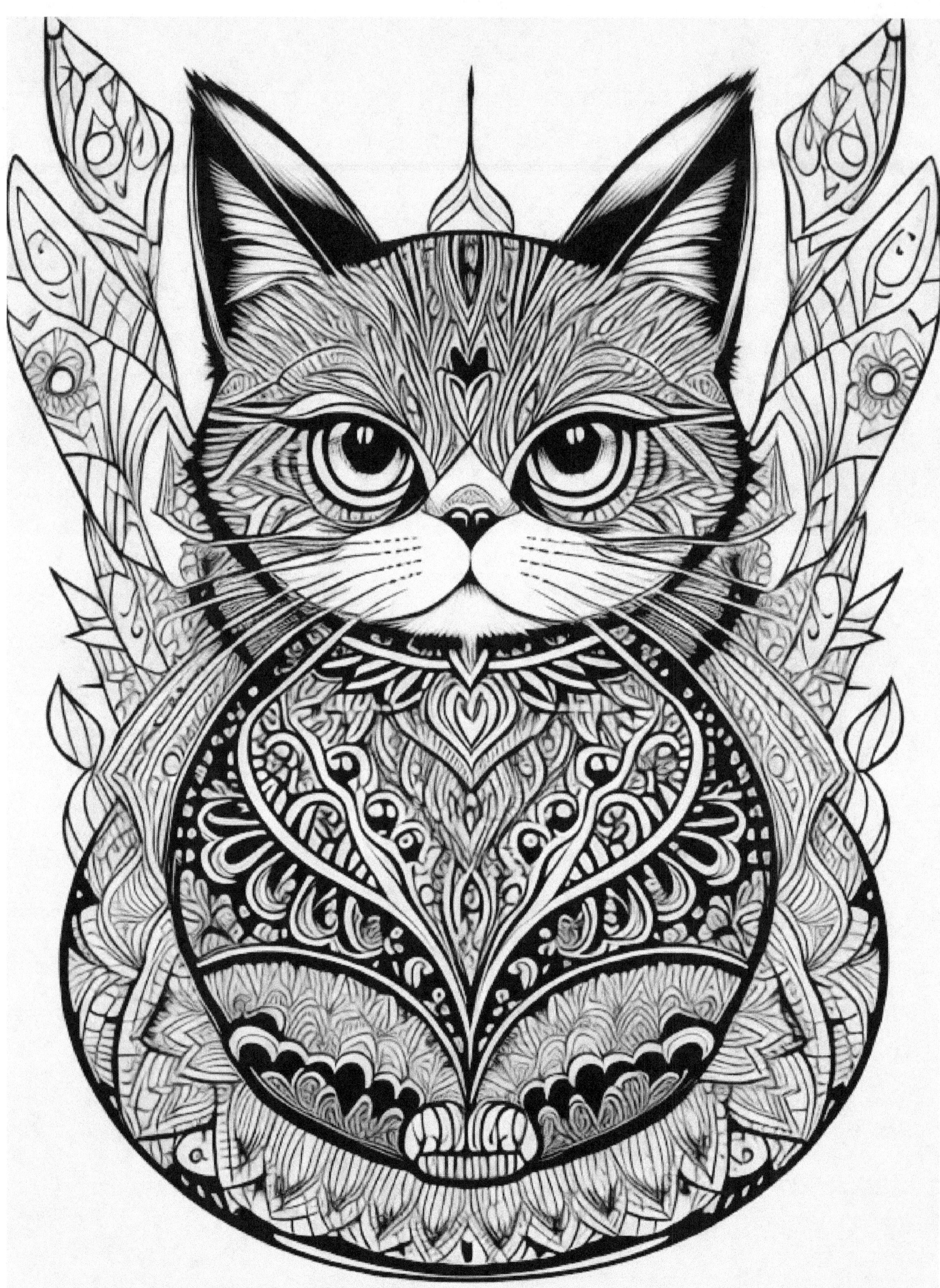

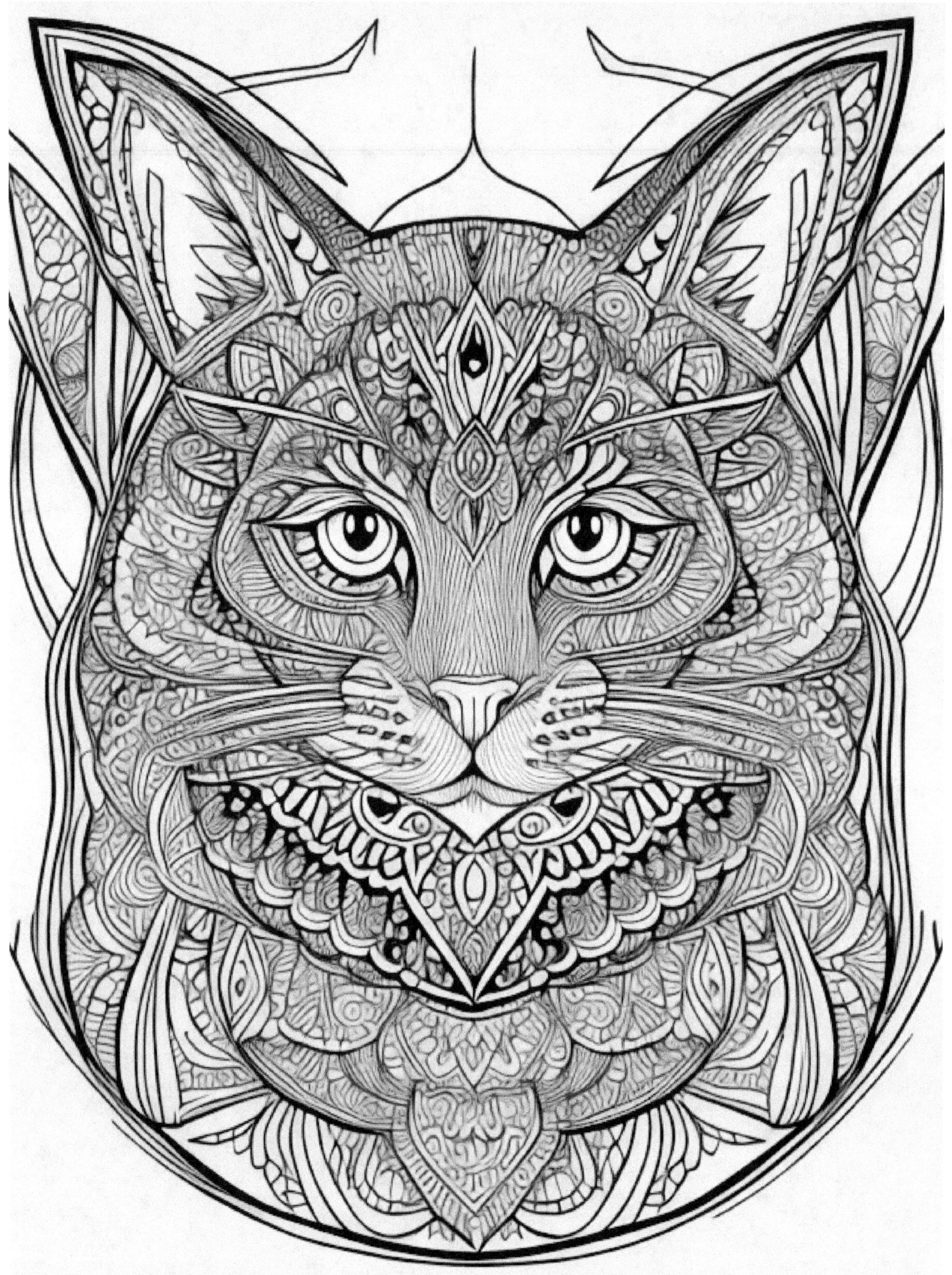

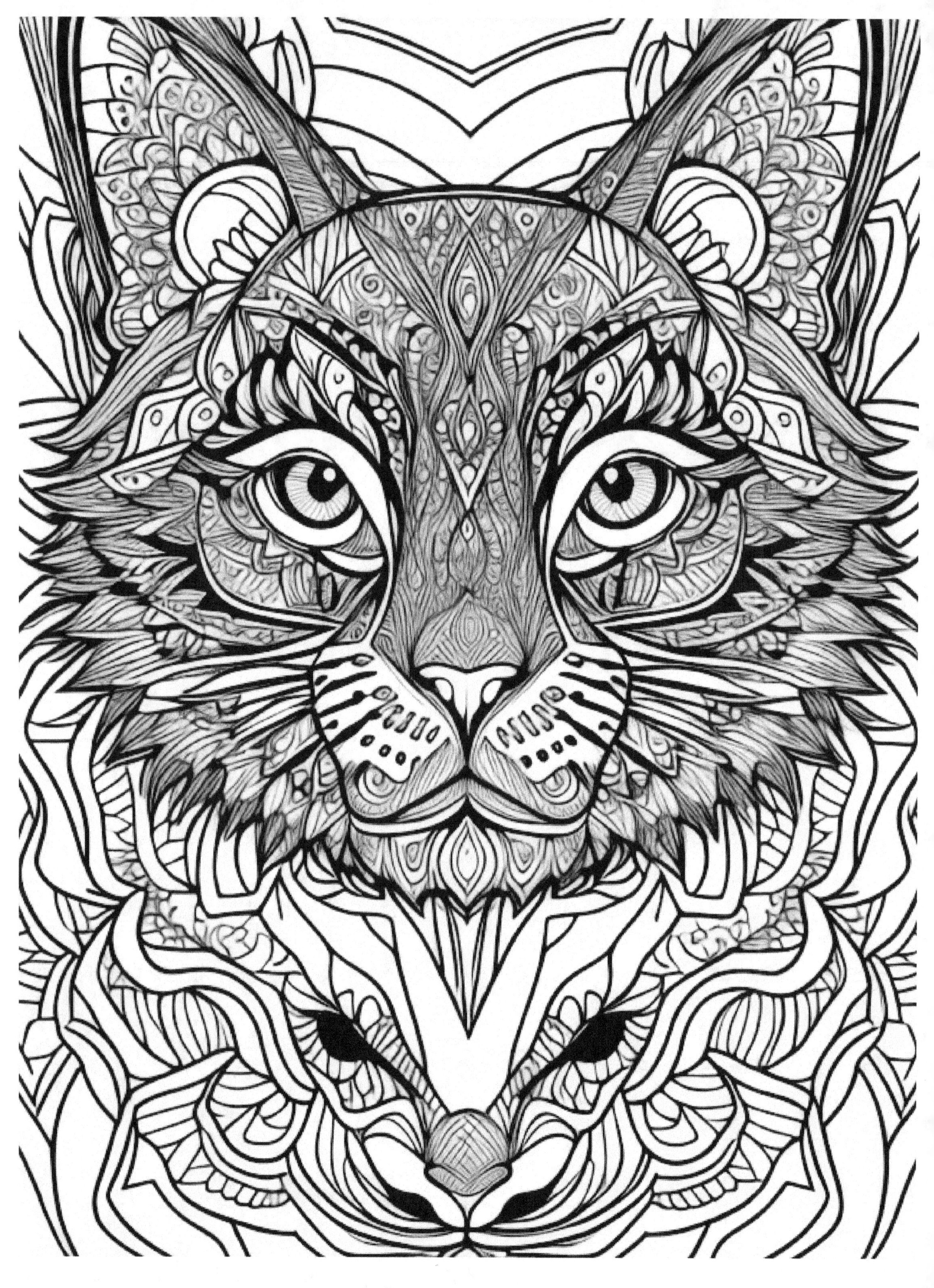

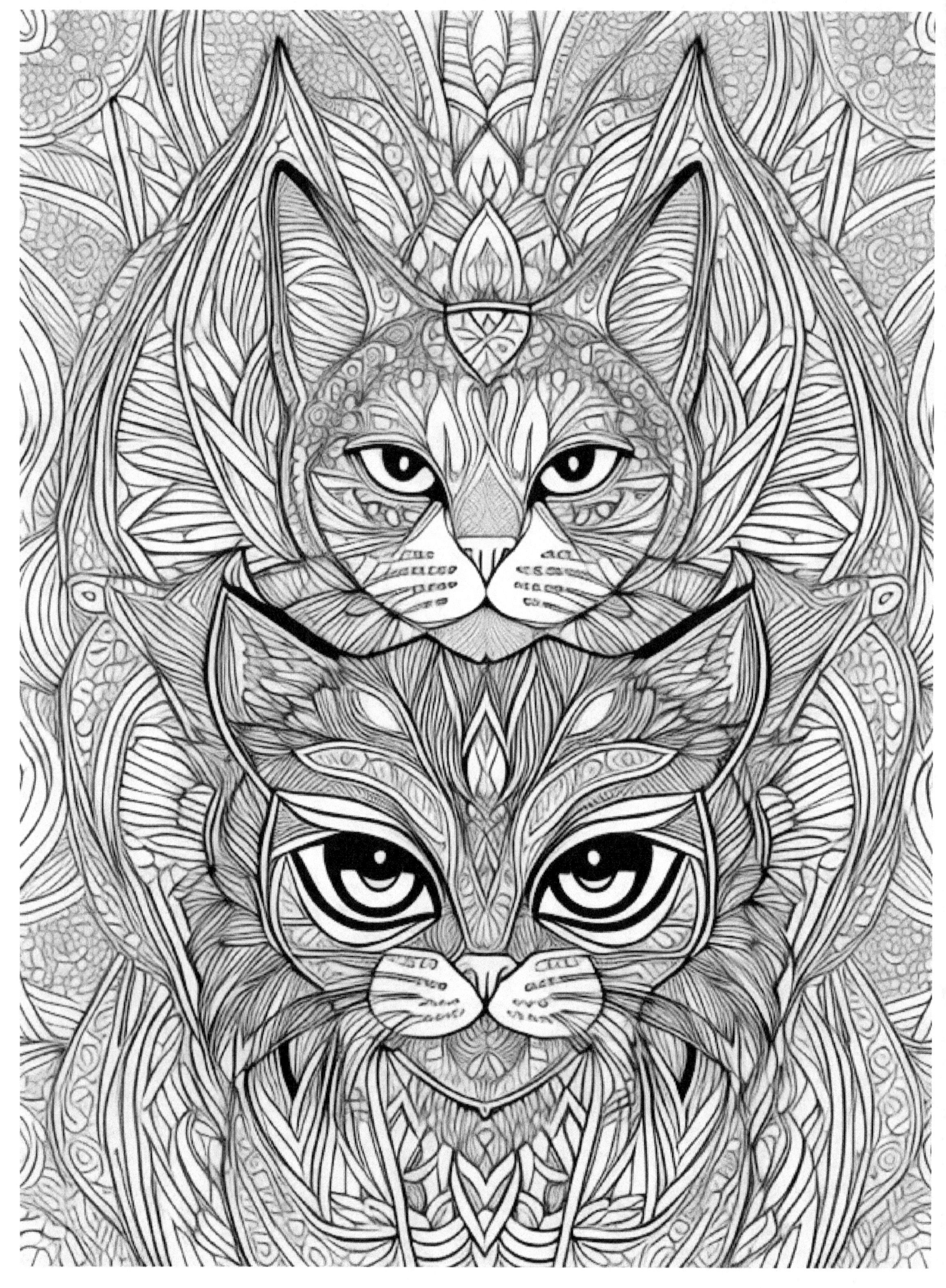

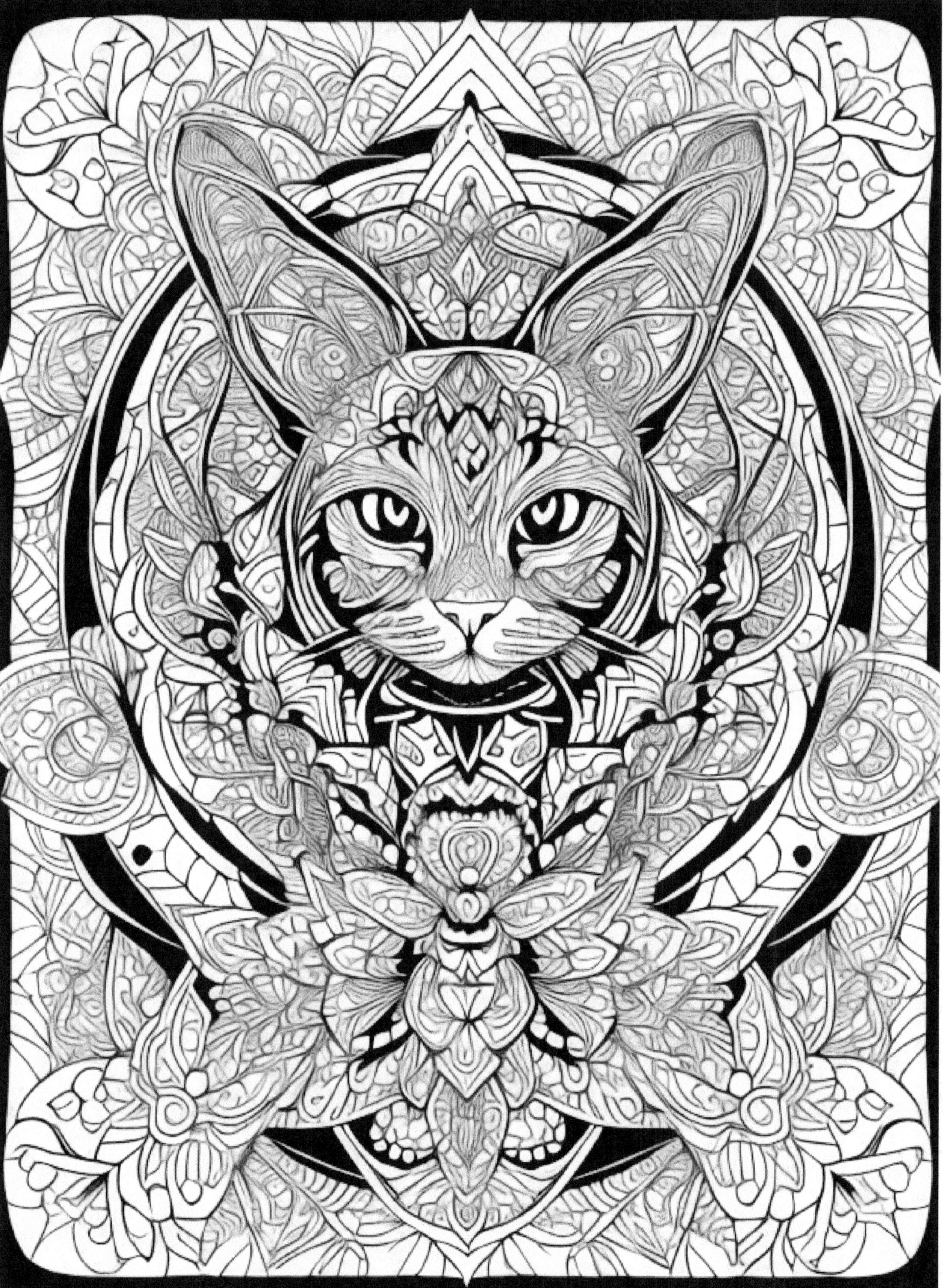

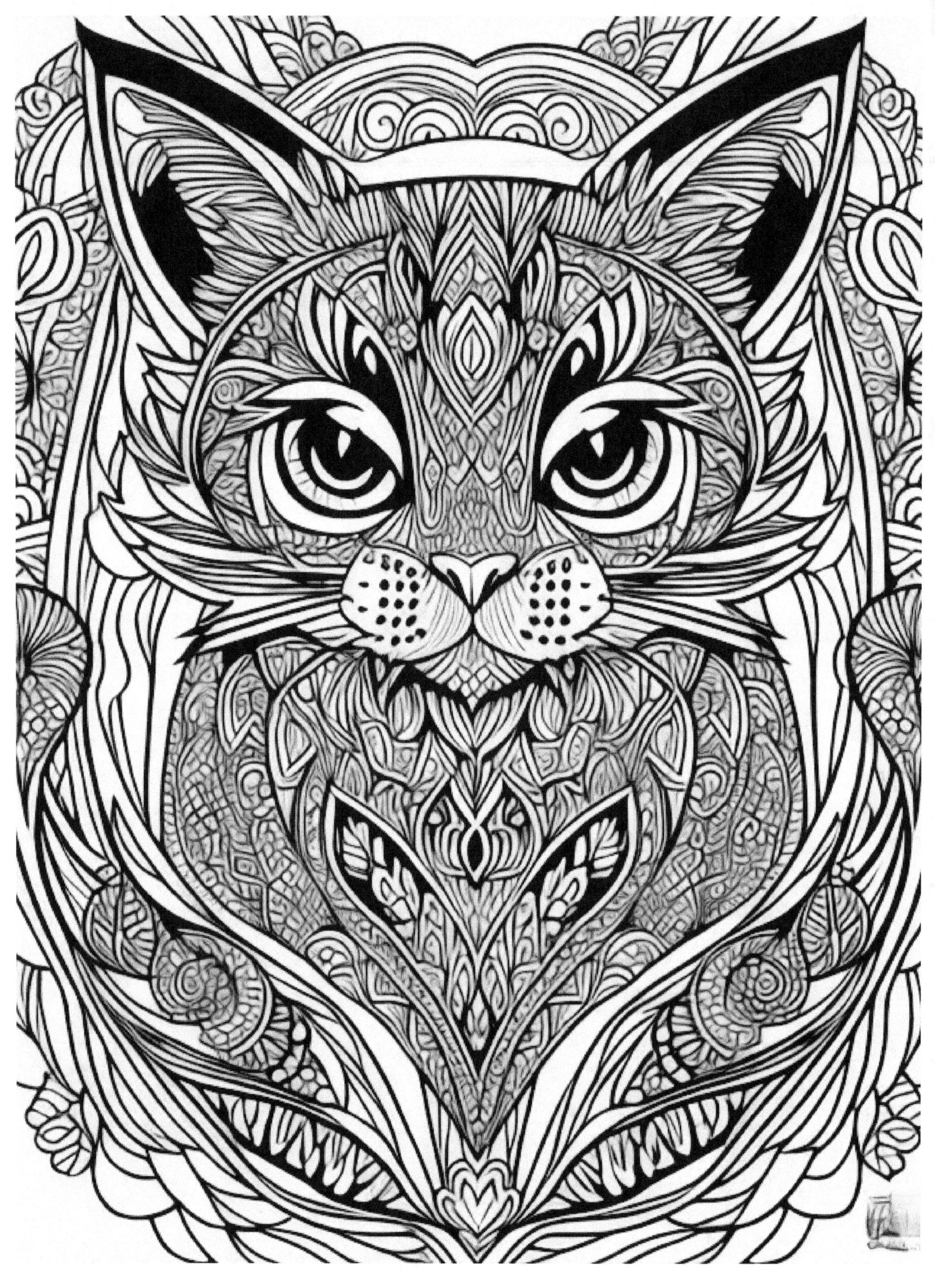

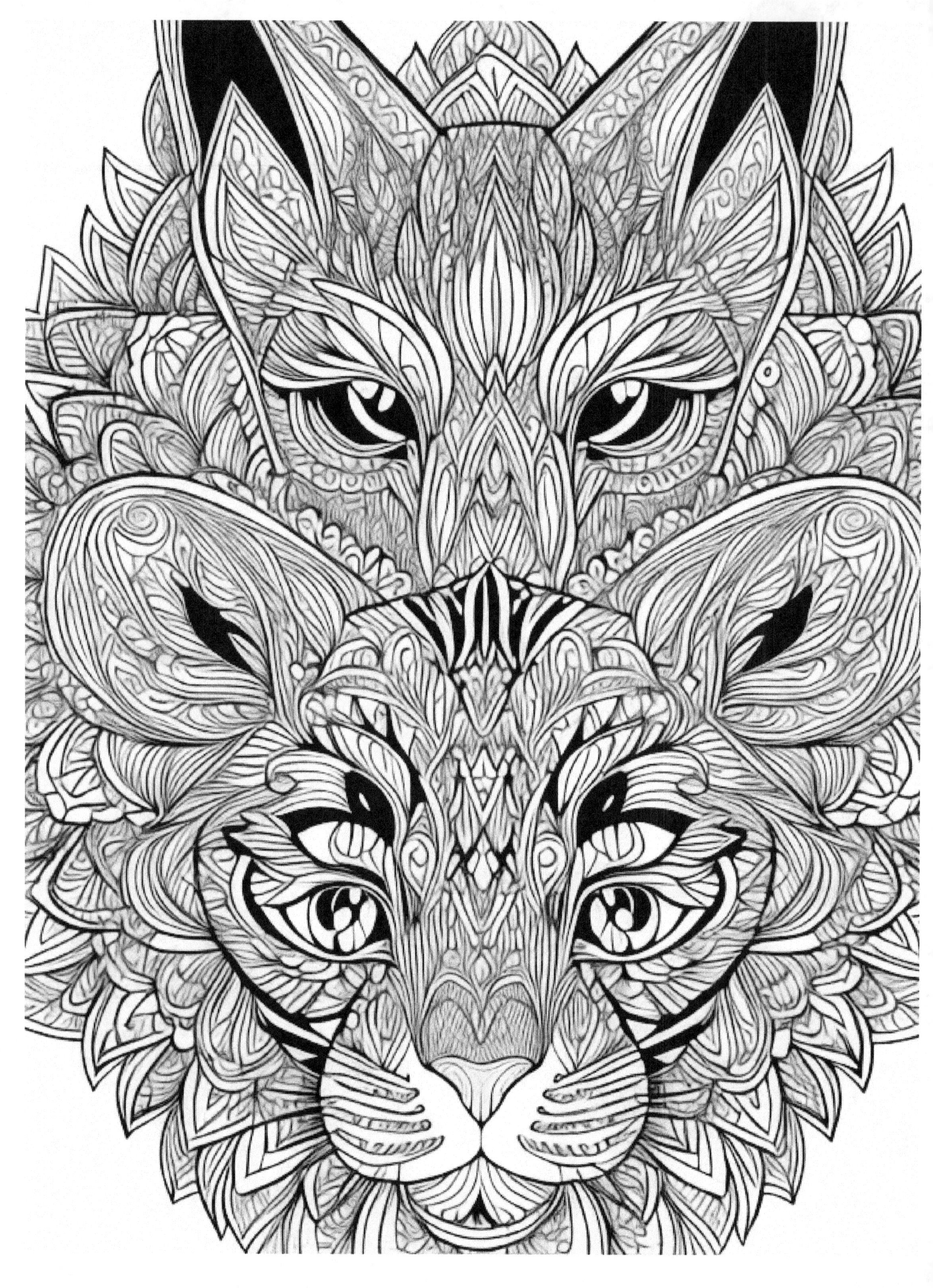

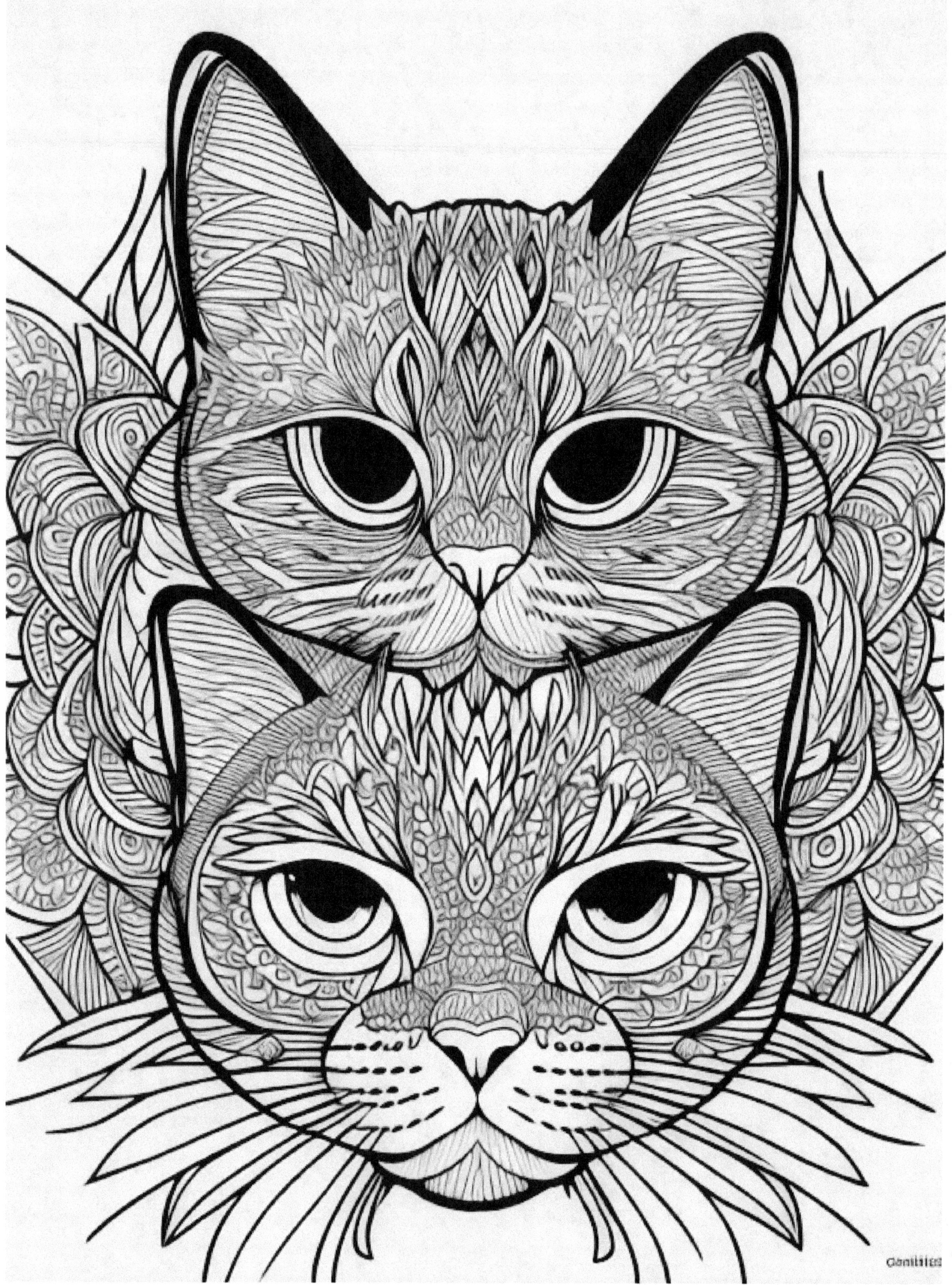

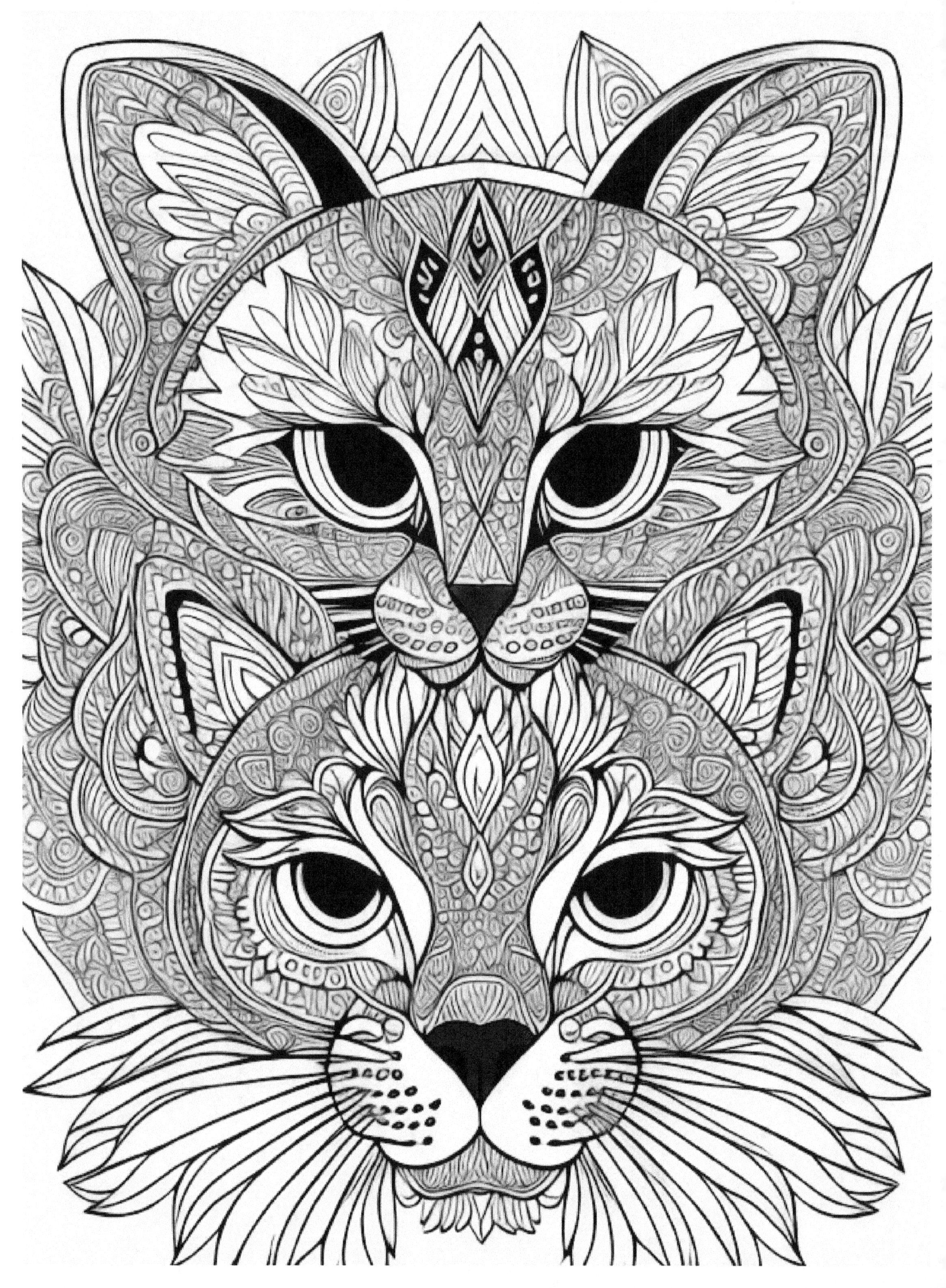

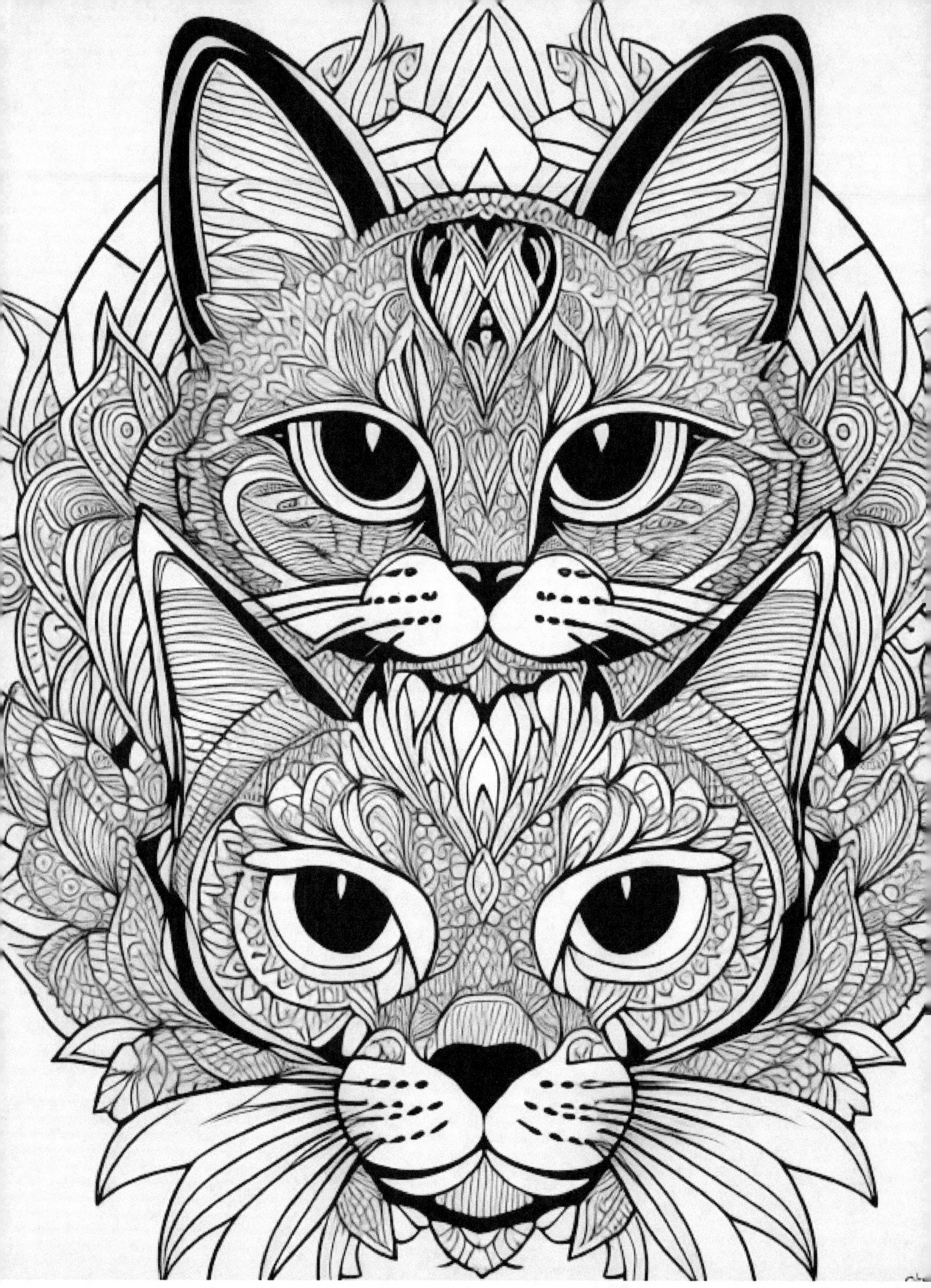

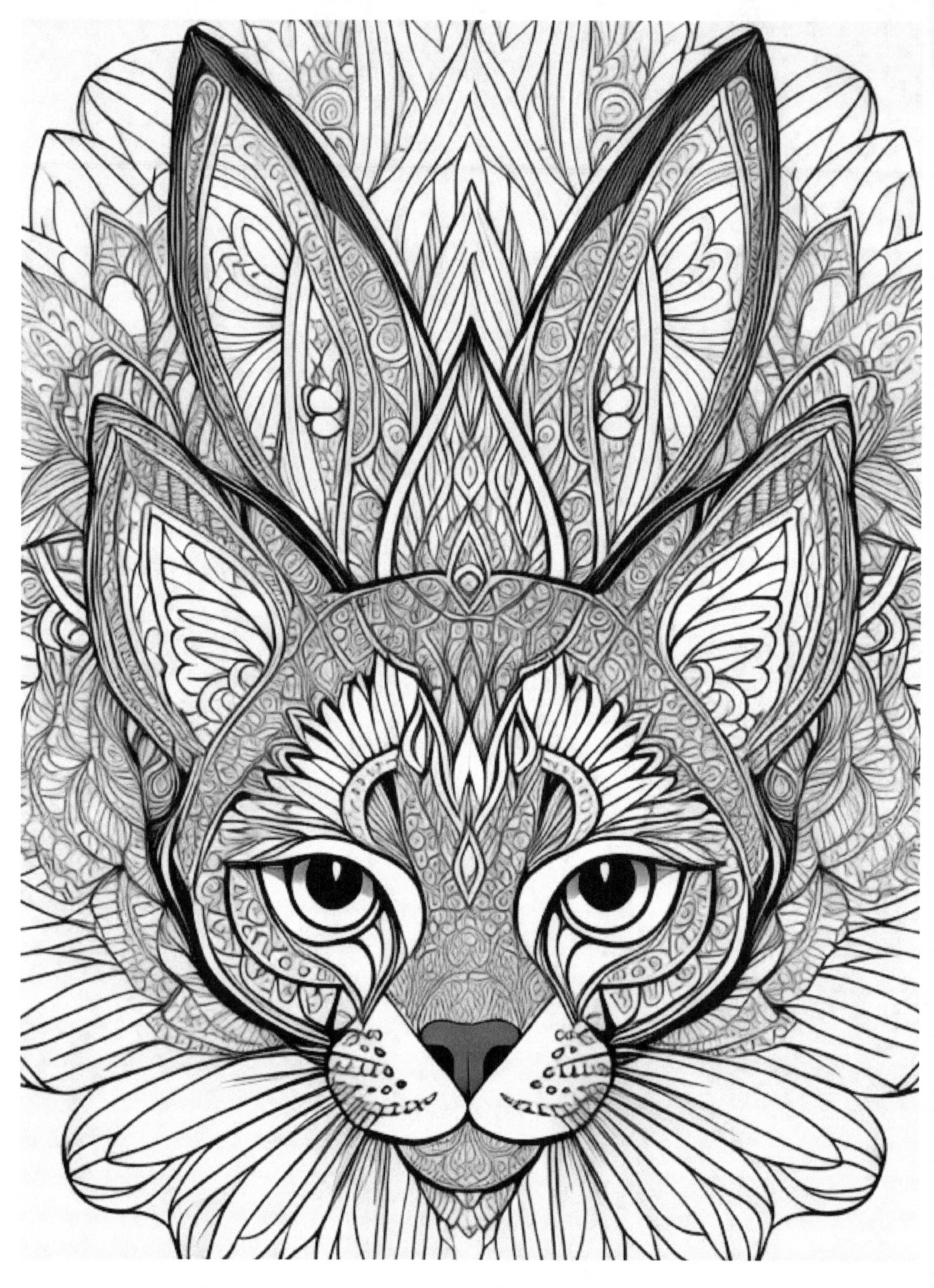

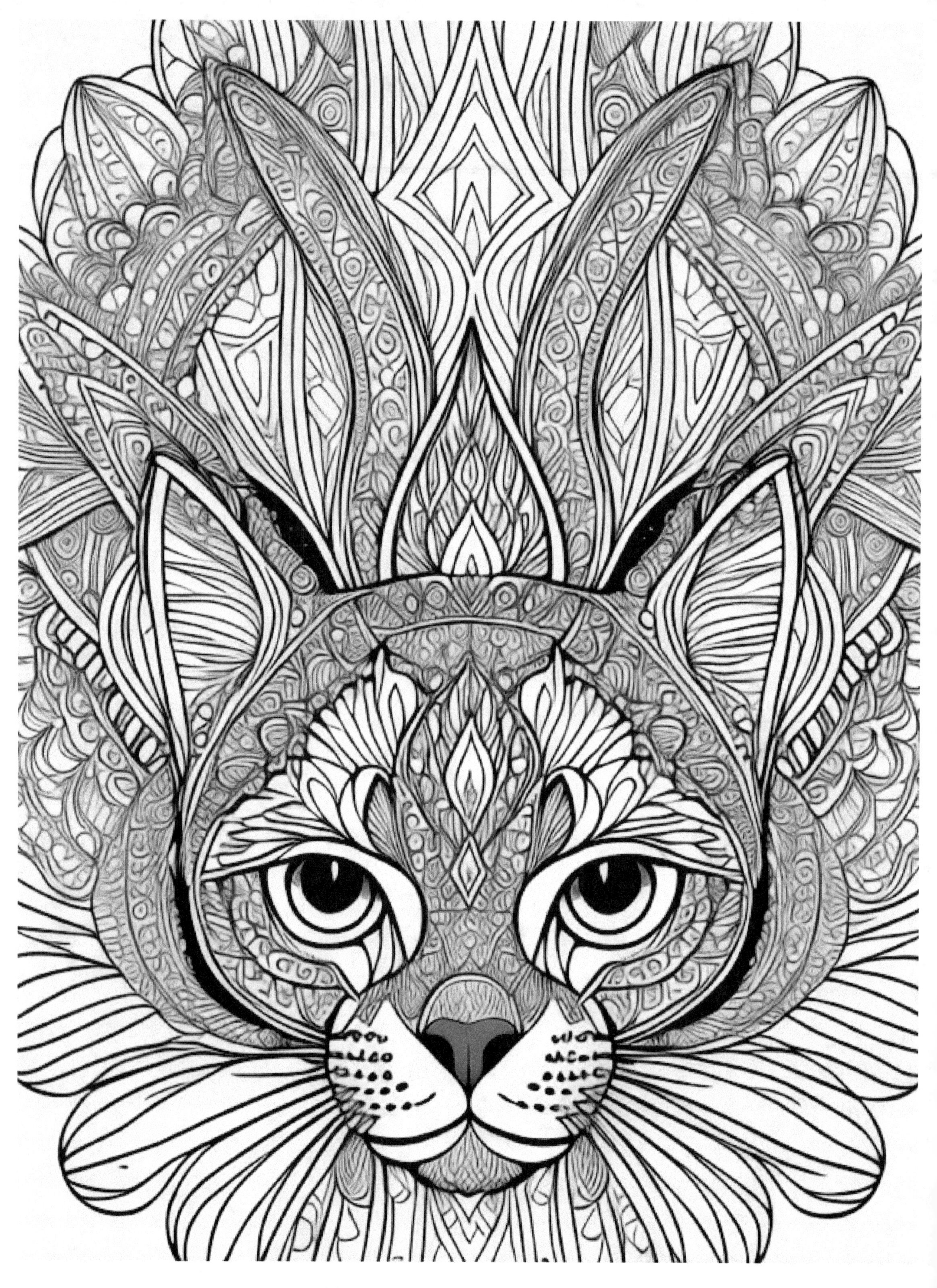

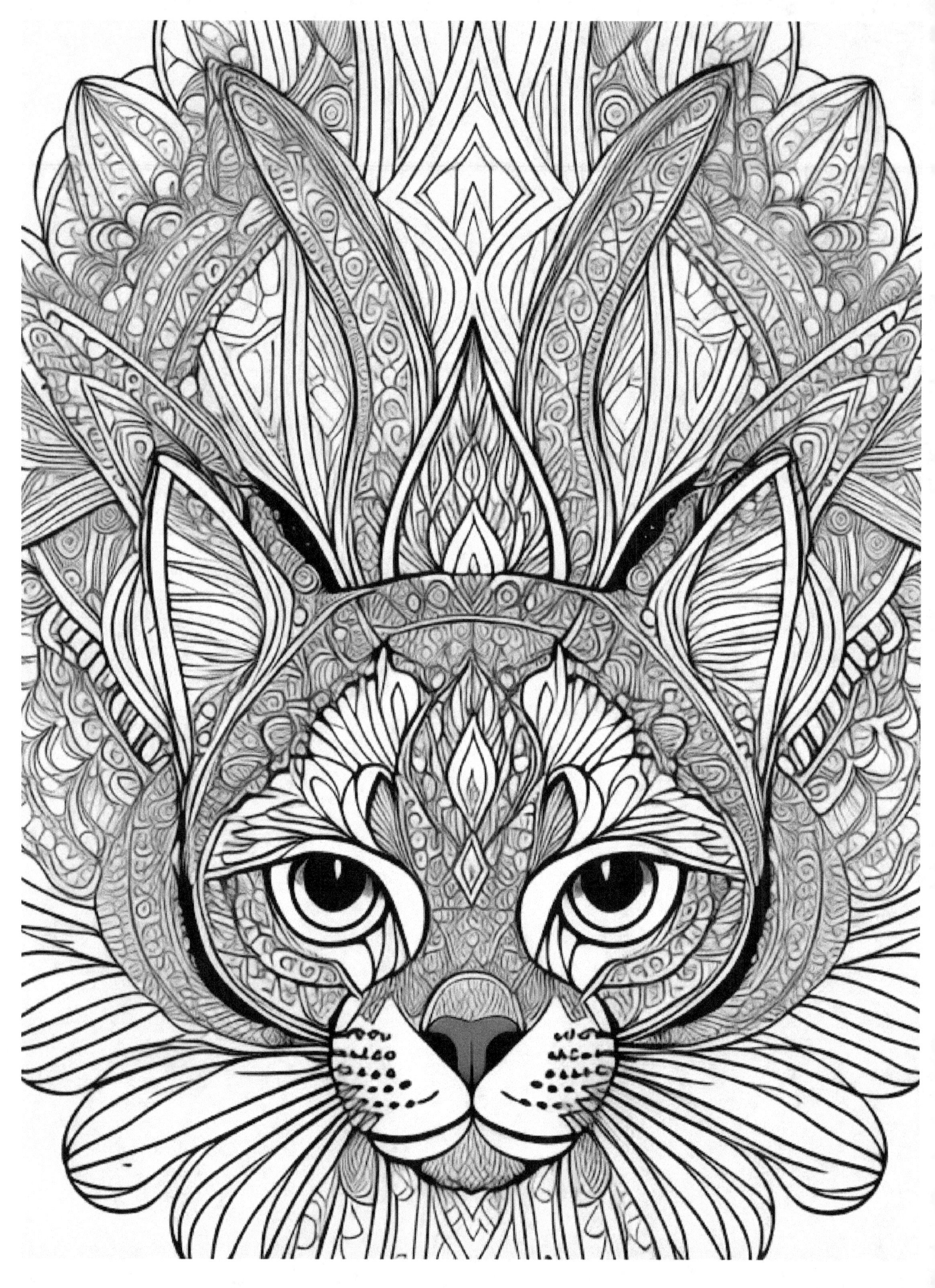

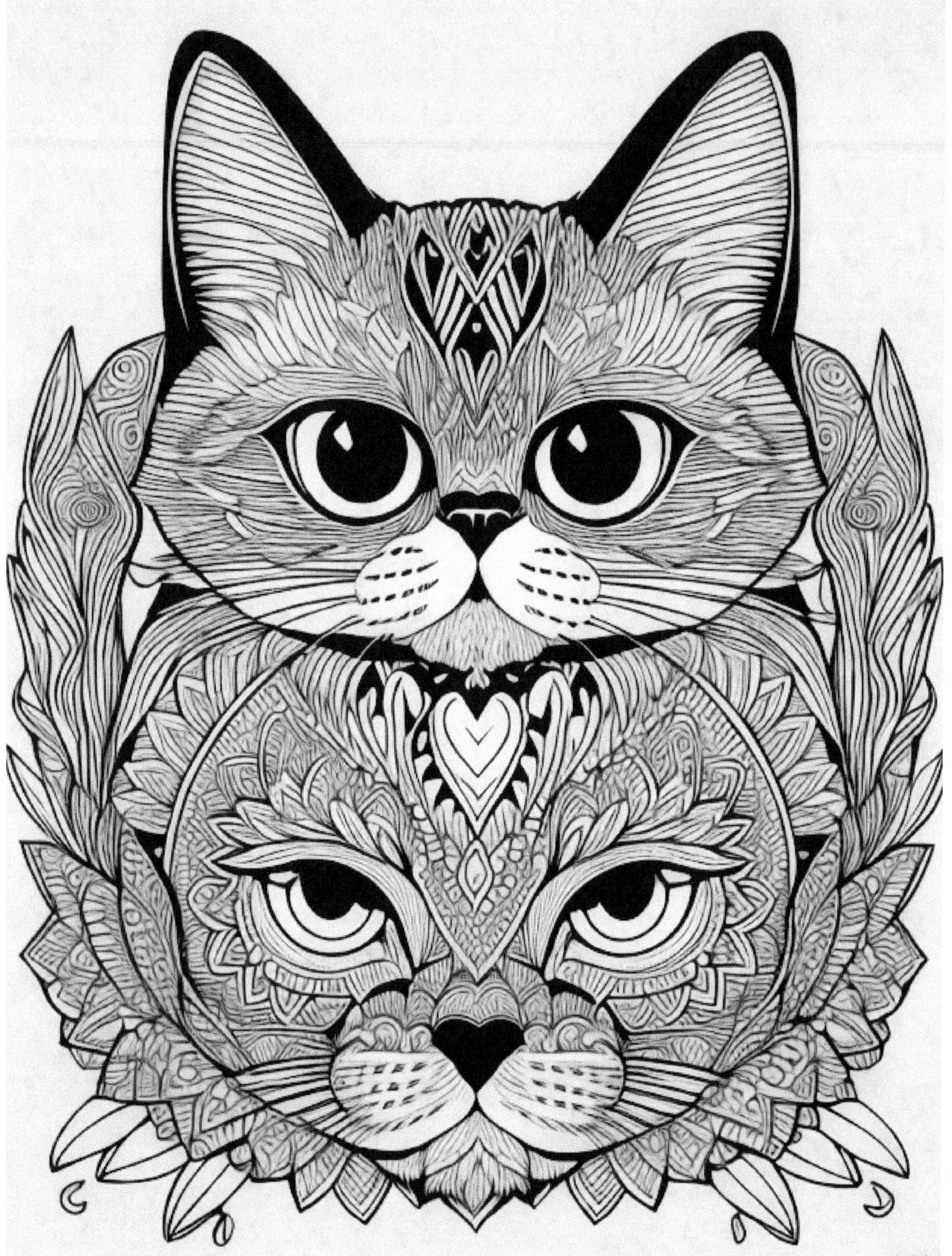

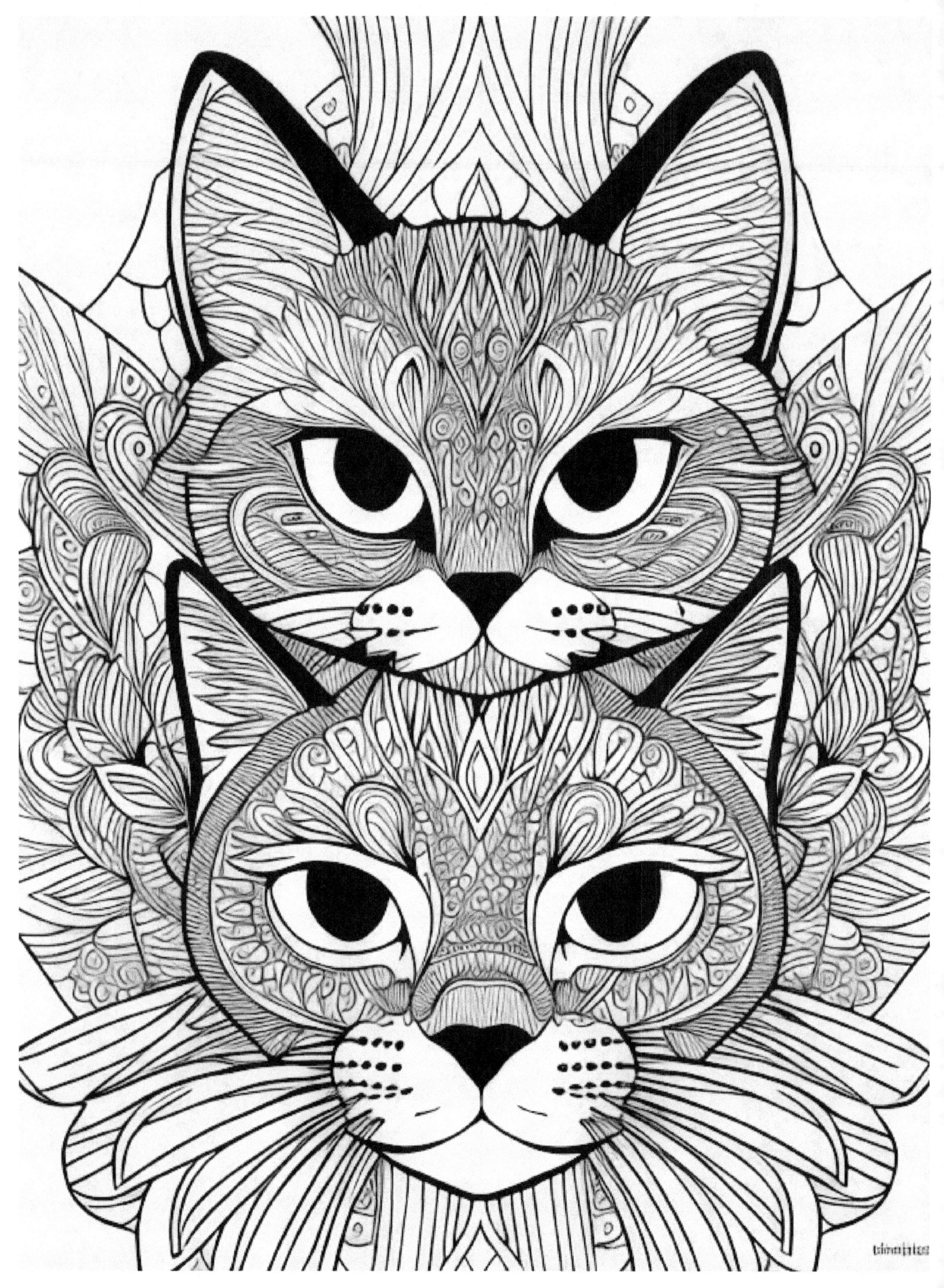

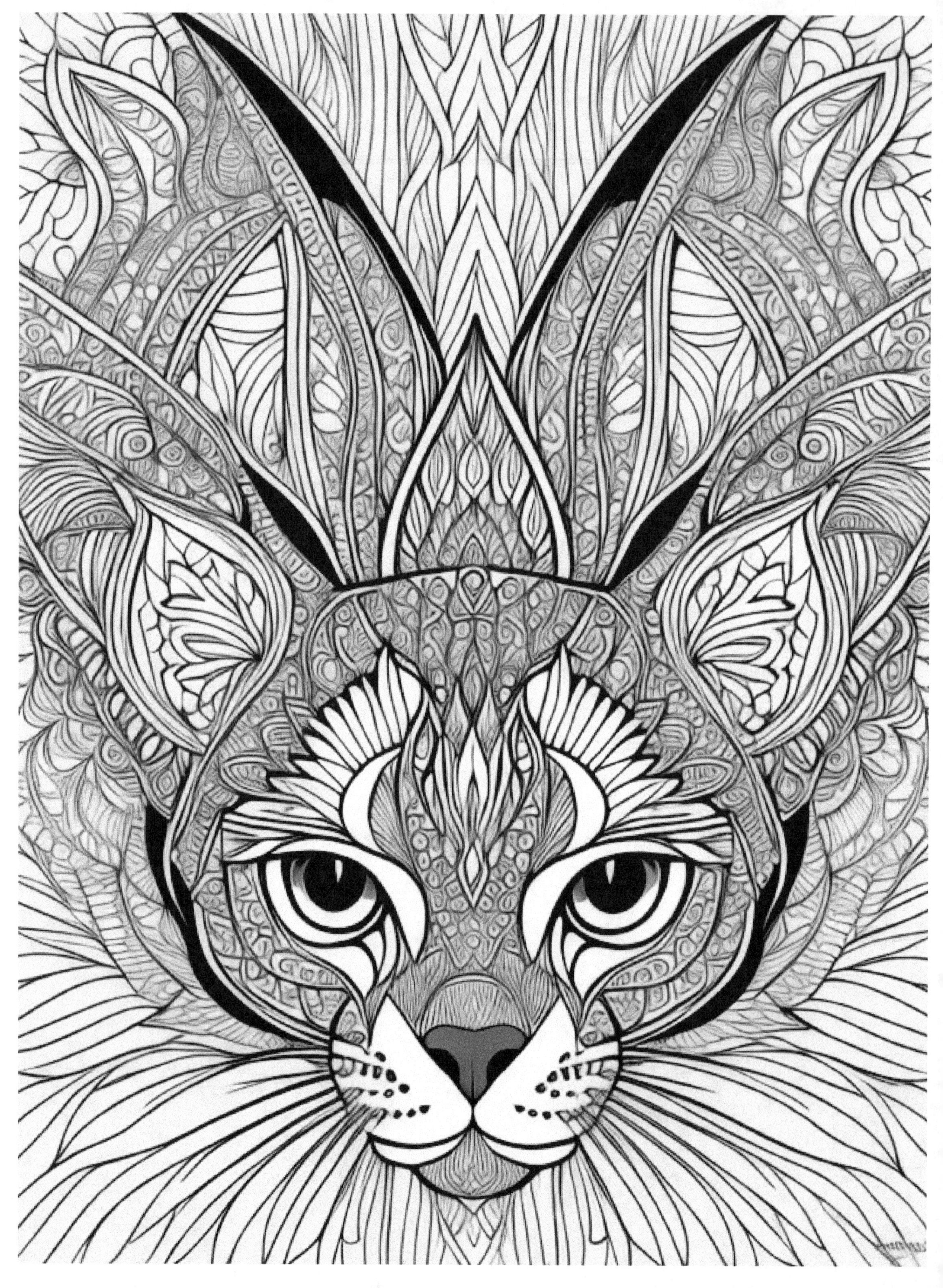

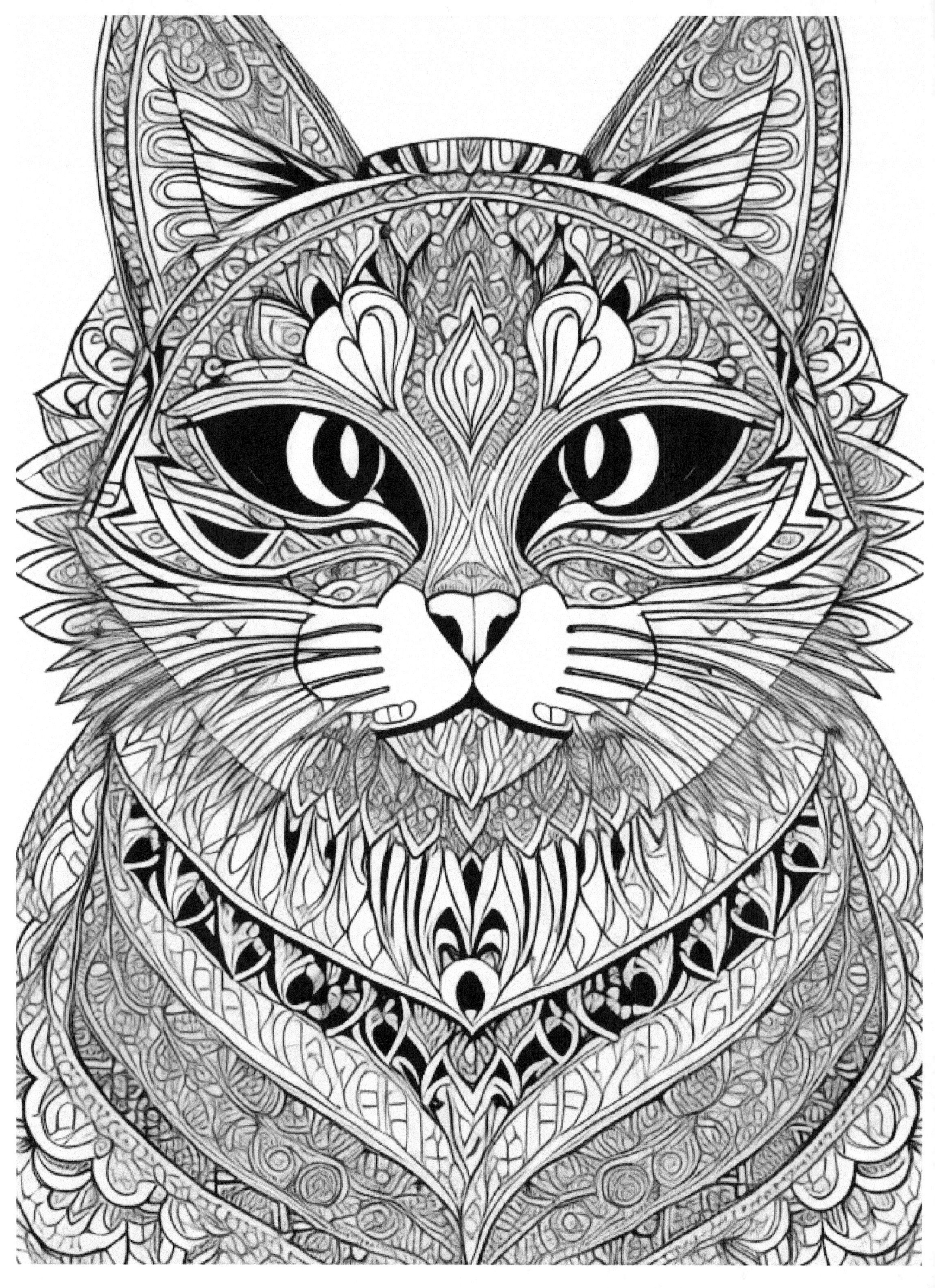

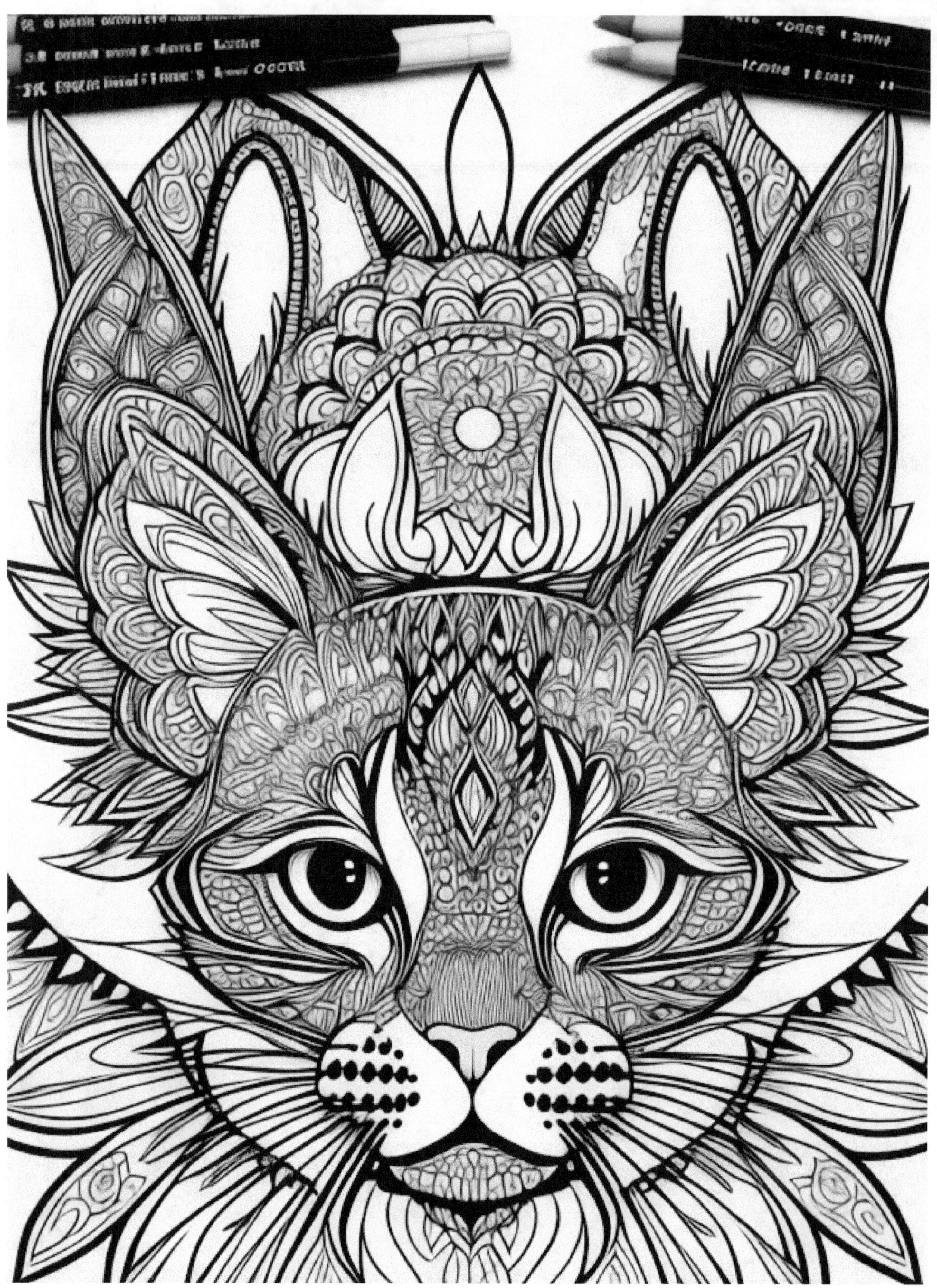

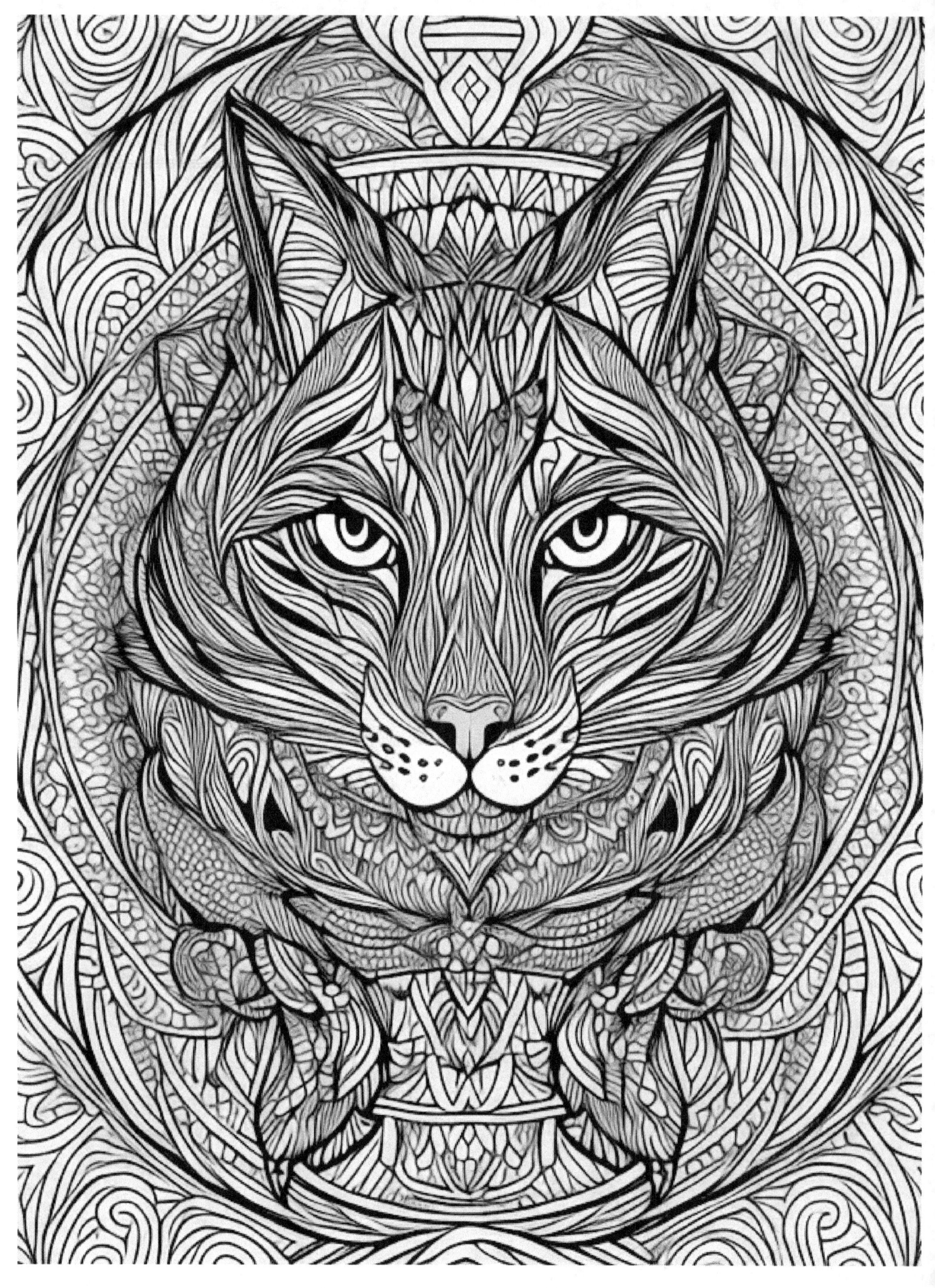

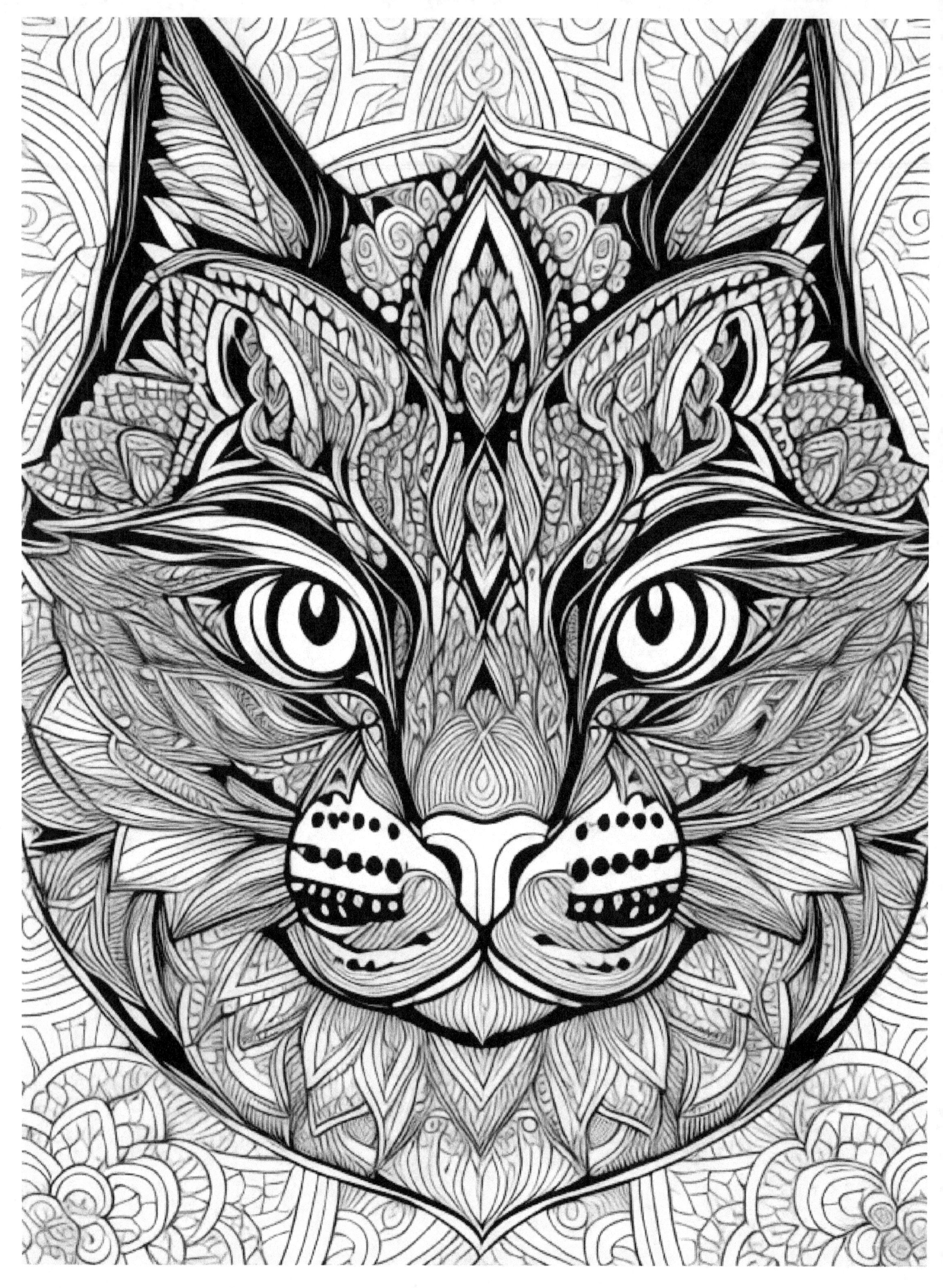

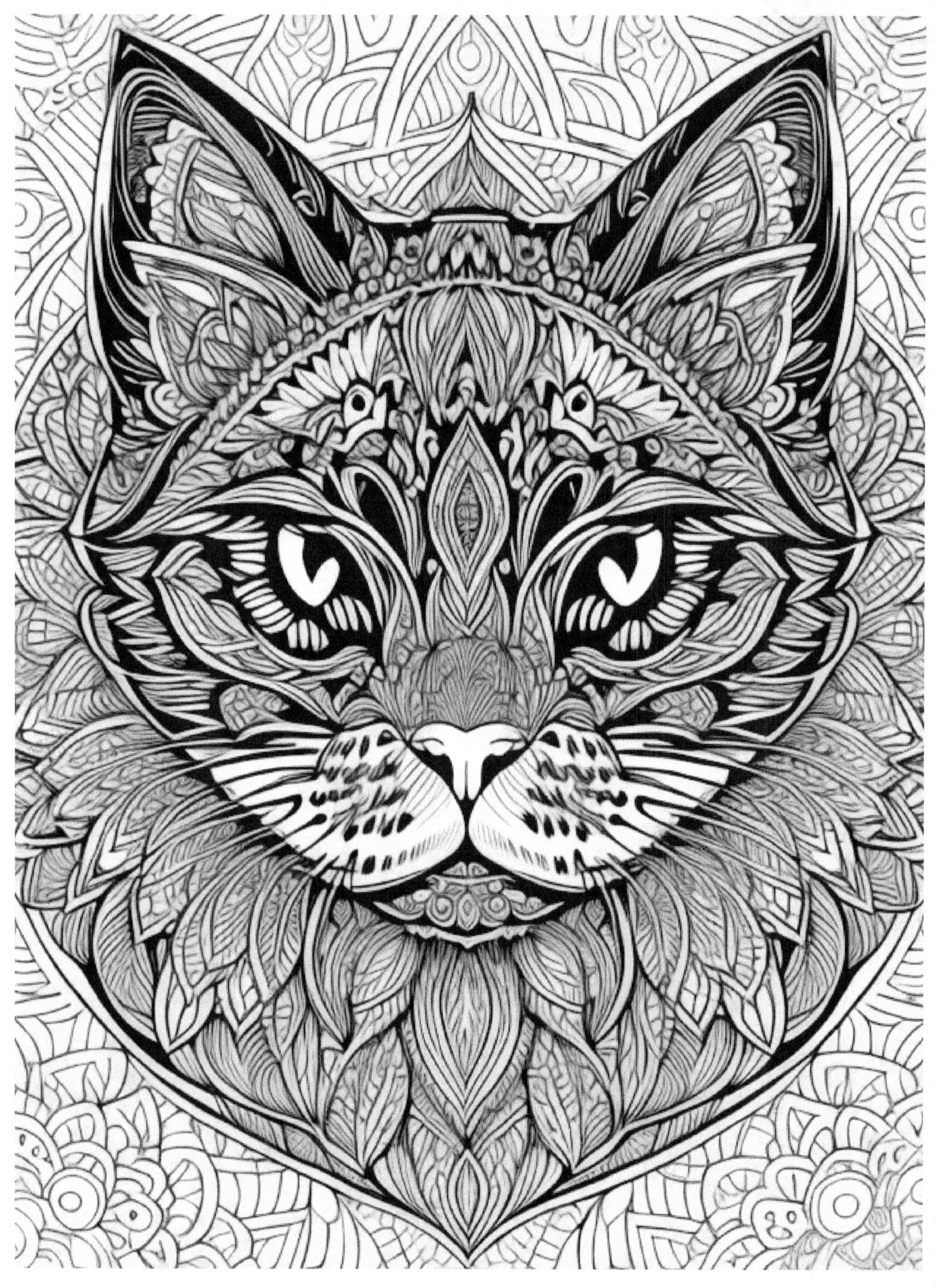

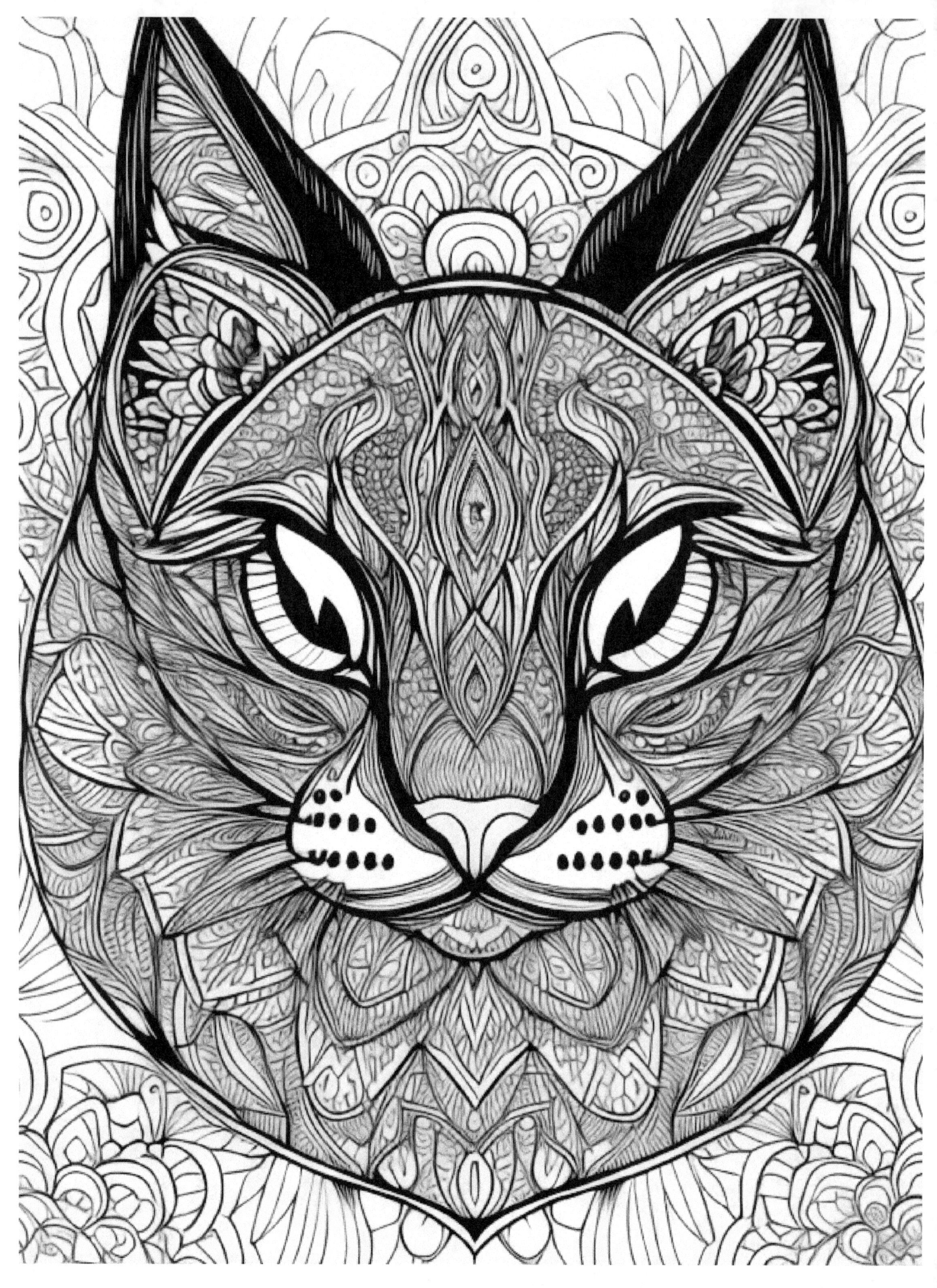

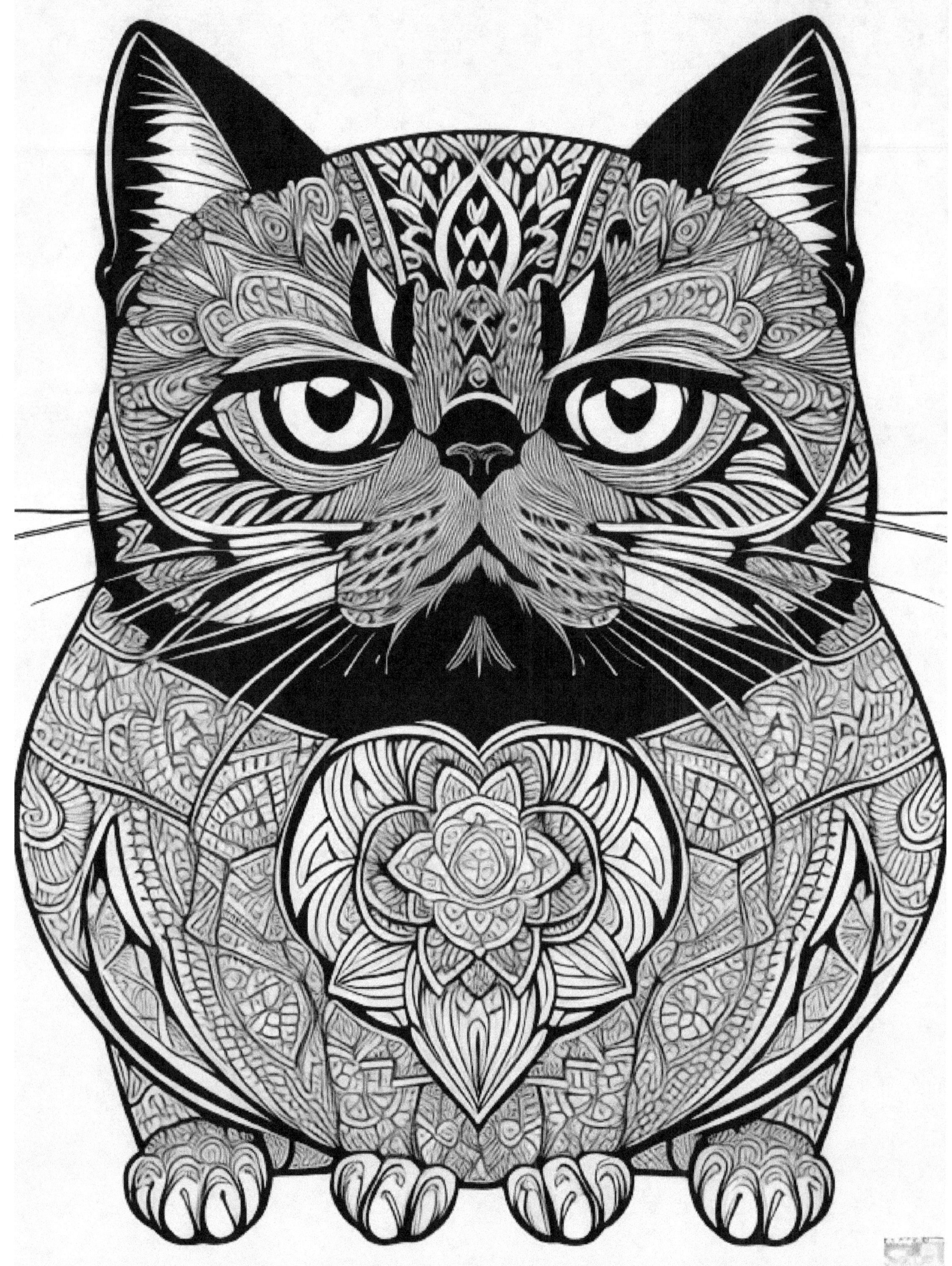

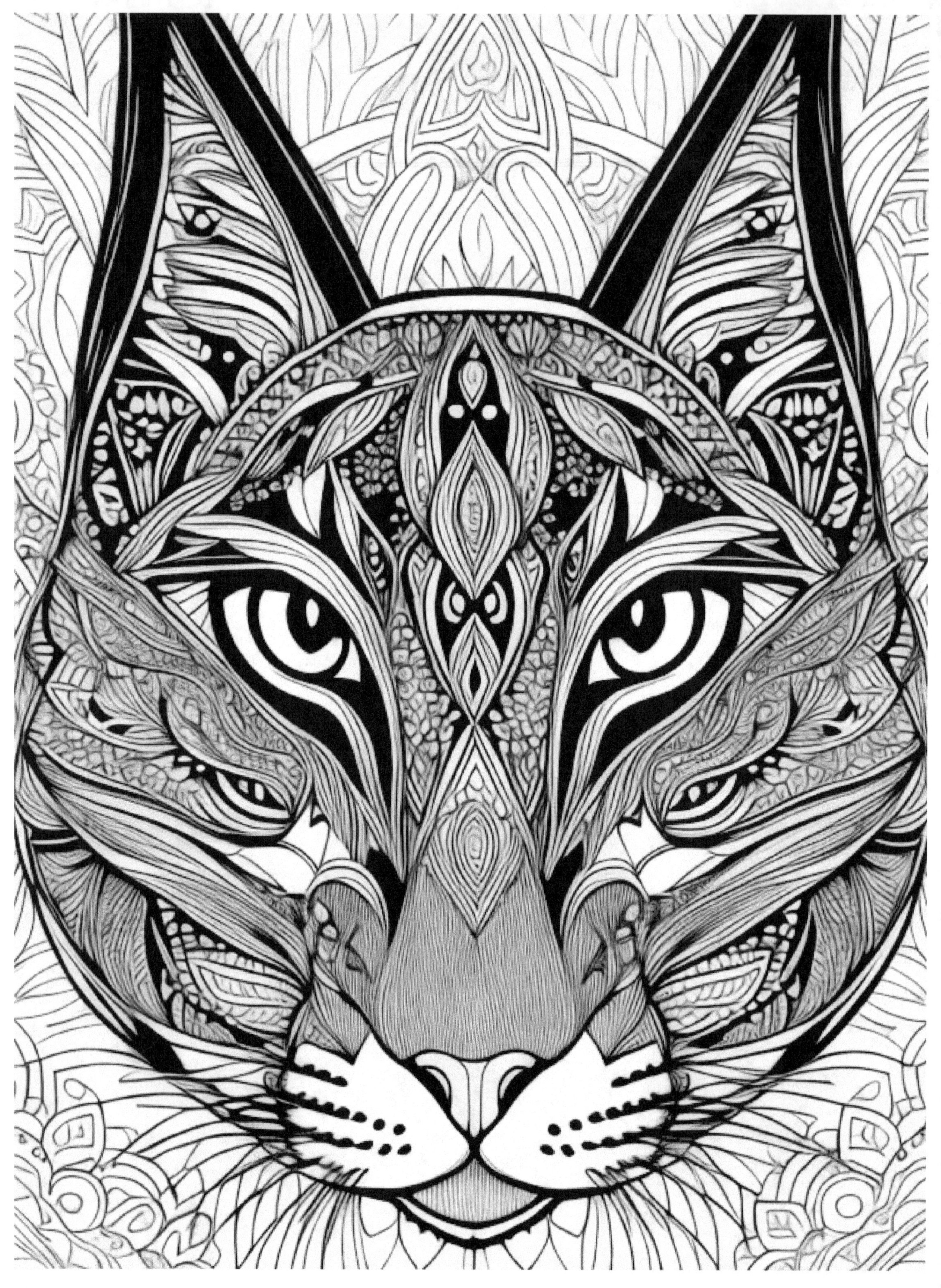

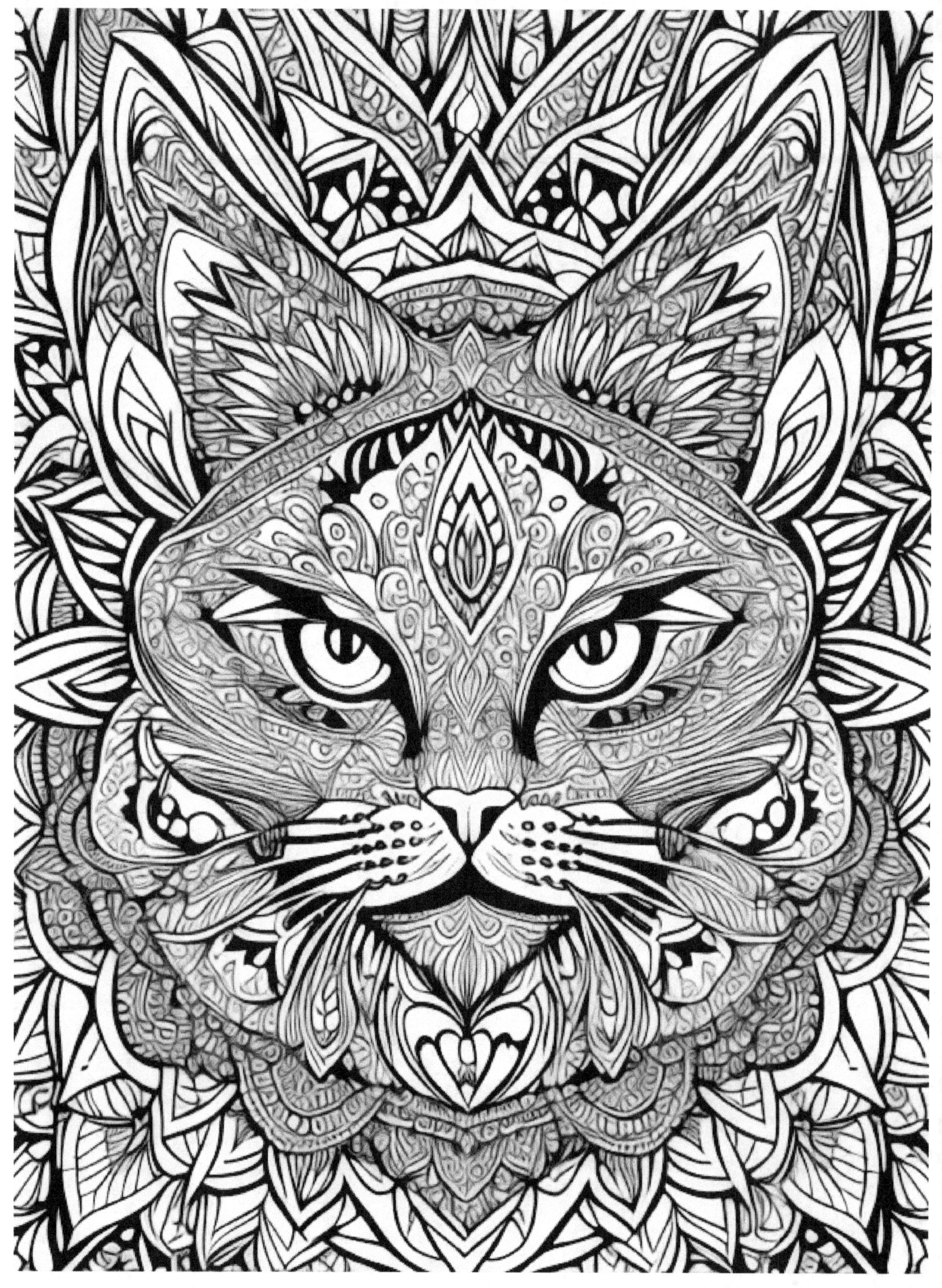

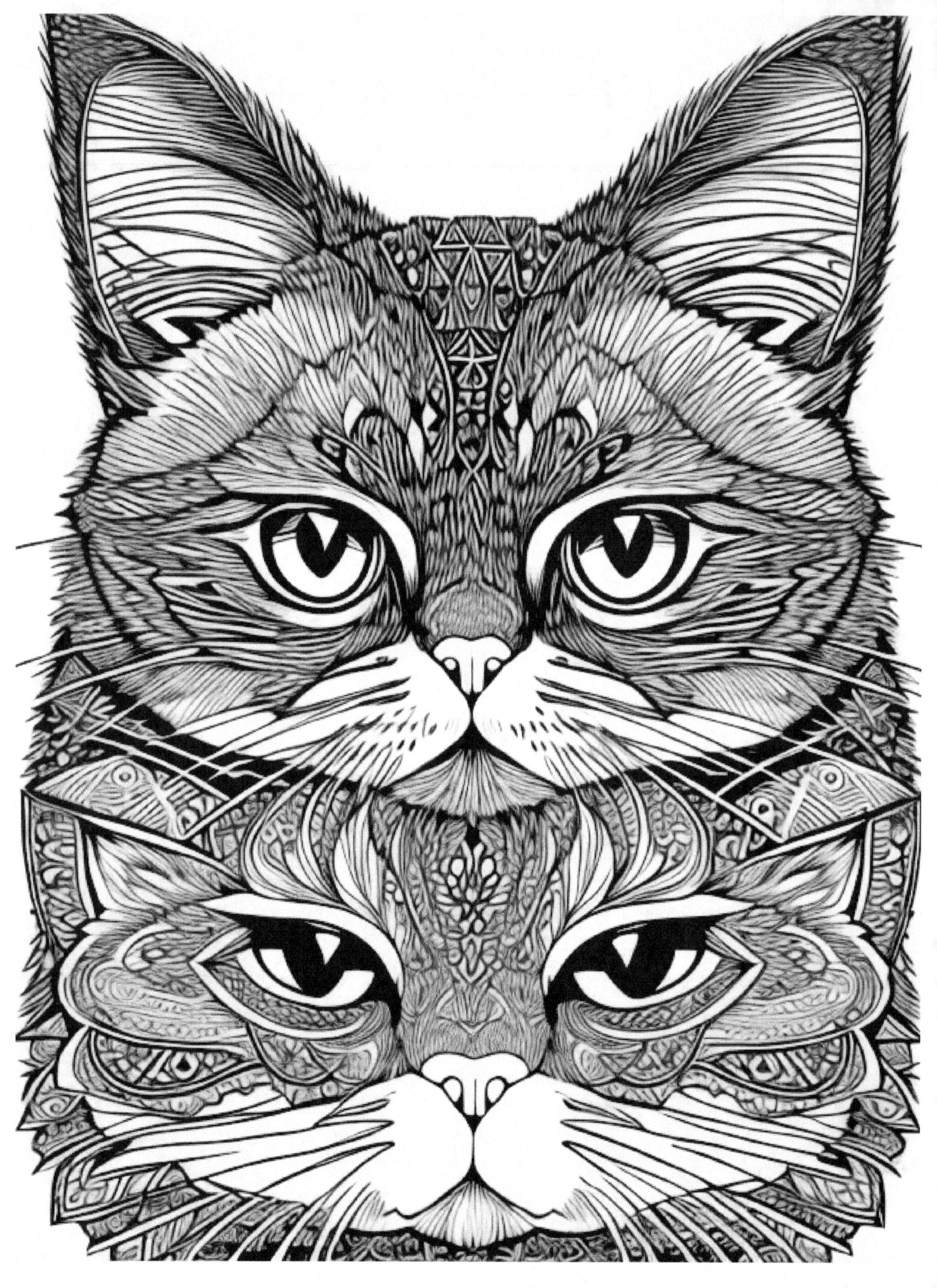